ENGLISH 1

a basic course for adults

LEARNER'S BOOK

ILONKA SCHMIDT MACKEY

Professor of Language Teaching Techniques
Department of Languages and Linguistics
Laval University

NEWBURY HOUSE PUBLISHERS

NEWBURY HOUSE PUBLISHERS, INC.

Language Science
Language Teaching
Language Learning

ROWLEY, MASSACHUSETTS 01969

ISBN   912066 25 3

illustrated by JESSICA M. MACDONALD

First printing: February 1972

Printed in the United States of America

UNIT 1

1.

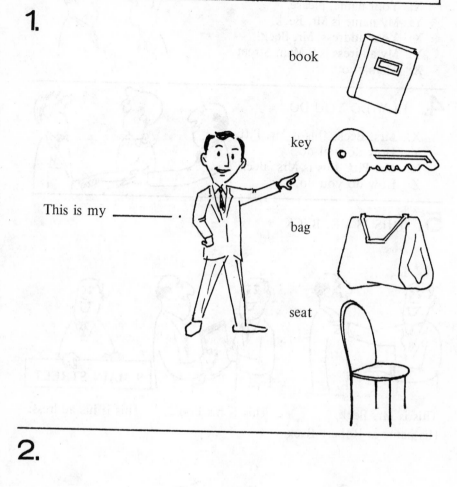

This is my _____ .

book

key

bag

seat

2.

Mr. Beck

Mrs. Beck

Miss Bennet

3. YOUR NAME, PLEASE

X: Your name, please.
Y: My name is Mr. Beck.
X: Your address, Mr. Beck.
Y: My address is 9 Main Street.
X: Thank you.

4. HOW DO YOU DO

X: Mrs. Beck, this is Mr. Pitt.
Y: How do you do.
X: Mr. Pitt, this is Mrs. Beck.
Z: How do you do.

5. THIS IS MR. BECK

This is Mr. Beck.   This is his book.   This is his address.
His name is Robert Beck.

That is Mrs. Beck.   That is her book.   That is her address.
Her name is Nelly Beck.

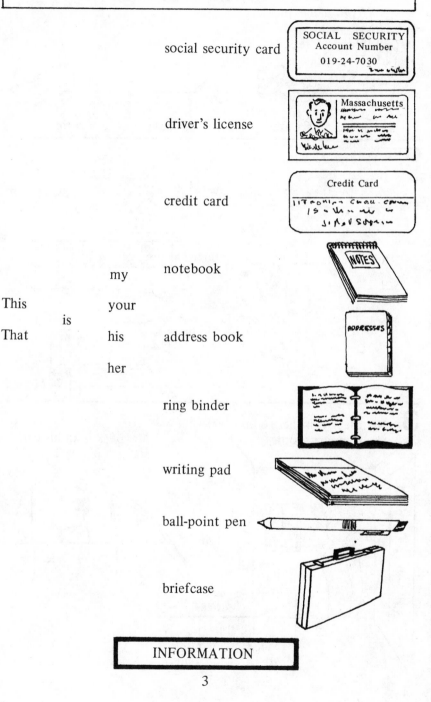

social security card

SOCIAL   SECURITY
Account Number
019-24-7030

driver's license

Massachusetts

credit card

Credit Card

notebook

NOTES

my

This

your
is
That   his   address book

her

ADDRESSES

ring binder

writing pad

ball-point pen

briefcase

INFORMATION

3

UNIT 2

1.

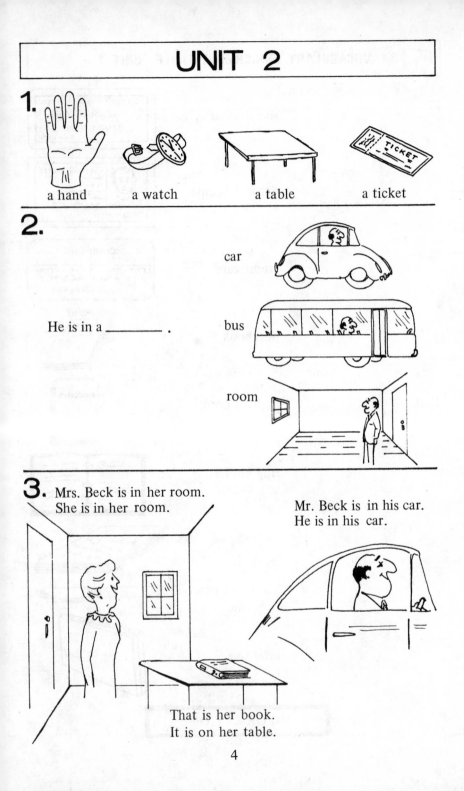

a hand   a watch   a table   a ticket

2.

car

He is in a _____ .   bus

room

3. Mrs. Beck is in her room.
She is in her room.

Mr. Beck is in his car.
He is in his car.

That is her book.
It is on her table.

4

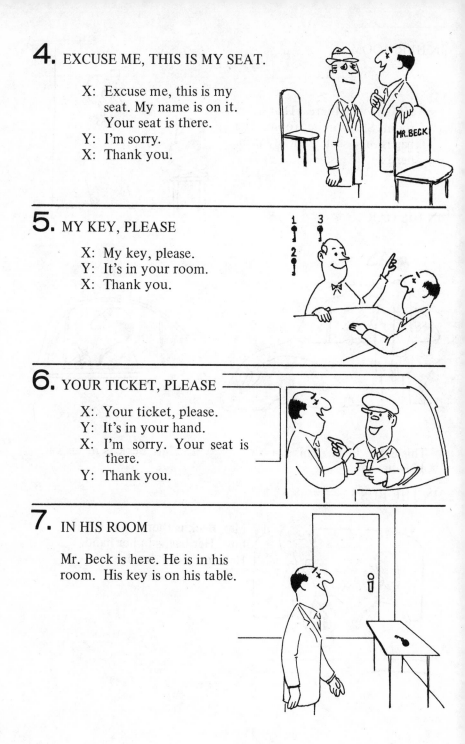

4. EXCUSE ME, THIS IS MY SEAT.

X: Excuse me, this is my seat. My name is on it. Your seat is there.
Y: I'm sorry.
X: Thank you.

5. MY KEY, PLEASE

X: My key, please.
Y: It's in your room.
X: Thank you.

6. YOUR TICKET, PLEASE

X: Your ticket, please.
Y: It's in your hand.
X: I'm sorry. Your seat is there.
Y: Thank you.

7. IN HIS ROOM

Mr. Beck is here. He is in his room. His key is on his table.

IN HER ROOM

Mrs. Beck is there. That is her room. She is in her room. Her bag is on a seat. Her key is in her bag.

IN HIS CAR

This is Mr. Beck. This is a car. It is his car.

Mr. Beck is in his car.

IN THE BUS

Mrs. Beck is there. She is in a bus. Her bag is in her hand. Her ticket is in her bag.

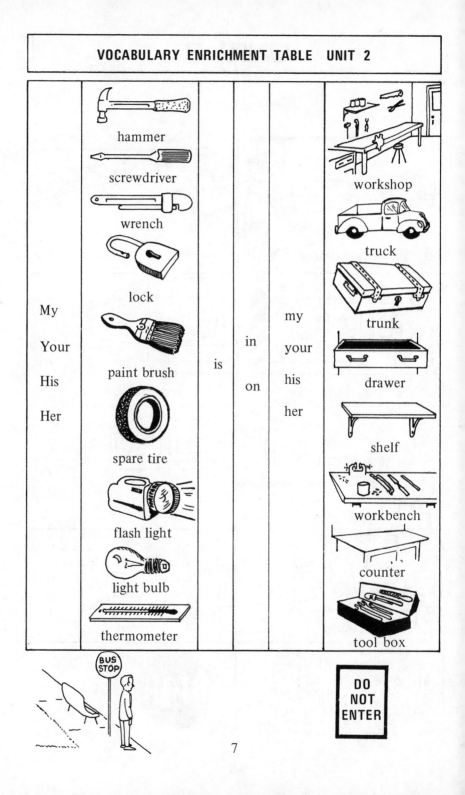

VOCABULARY ENRICHMENT TABLE   UNIT 2

	hammer			
	screwdriver			workshop
	wrench			truck
	lock			trunk
My	paint brush	is	my	drawer
Your		in	your	
His		on	his	shelf
Her	spare tire		her	workbench
	flash light			counter
	light bulb			
	thermometer			tool box

BUS STOP

DO NOT ENTER

7

UNIT 3

1.

He
She is going to the _____.

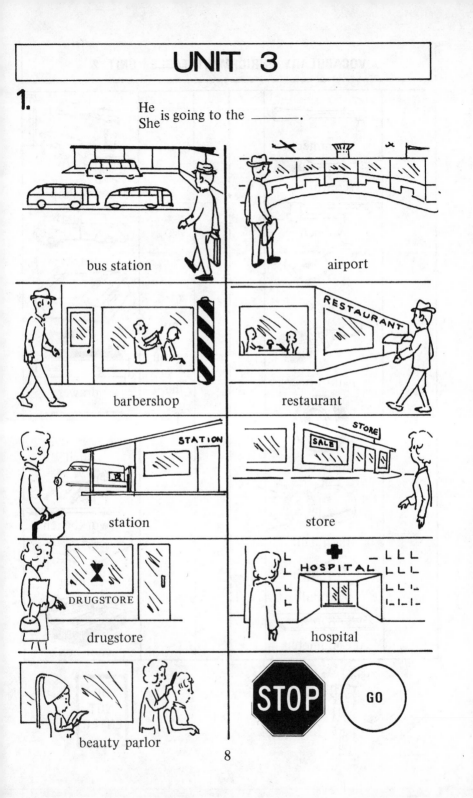

bus station

airport

barbershop

restaurant

station

store

drugstore

hospital

beauty parlor

STOP   GO

8

2.

That's the airport.　　　That's the bus station.

This is the bus station.

3. SEE YOU LATER.

X: Hello, Robert.
Y: Hello, Ted, how are you?
X: Fine, thanks. How are you?
Y: Fine. I'm going to the barbershop.
X: I'm going to the drugstore. That's my bus. Sorry, Robert, see you later.
Y: Good-bye, Ted.

4. GOING TO BOSTON

Mrs. Beck is in the bus. Her bag is on the seat. It is seat five. Her ticket is in her hand. She is going to Boston.

GOING TO THE BUS STATION

Mr. Beck is in Boston. He is in his car. He is going to the bus station.

9

I am
You are
going to the _____ .

subway	library	university	theater
show	concert	dance	party
wedding	funeral	reception	club
meeting	convention	country	beach

UNIT 4

1.

What's that?
It's my ticket.

What time is it?
It's two o'clock.

What's in your bag?
My books are in my bag.

What's this?
It's a telephone.
These are numbers.

18 4835
This is my license number.

385-54-8529
This is my social security number.

2.

one table   two tables

one book   three books

one page   four pages

one ticket   five tickets

one key

six keys

11

3.

 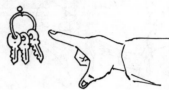

These are keys.   Those are keys.

4. THE TELEPHONE NUMBER

X: What's your name, please?
Y: My name's Mr. Beck. Mr. Robert Beck.
X: What's your telephone number, Mr. Beck?
Y: 953-9435.
X: What's your social security number?
Y: 957-34-8613.
X: Thank you, Mr. Beck.

5. IN THE BUS STATION

Mr. and Mrs. Beck are in the bus
station. Mr. Beck is going to New
York.
"What time is it, Robert?"
"It's four."
They are going to Bus 19. Bus
19 is going to New York.
"Your ticket, please."
"My ticket is here. Those are my
my bags."

Mr. Beck is in the bus. His seat
number is number eleven. Mrs.
Beck is in the station.
"Good-bye, Robert."
"Good-bye, Nelly."

12

VOCABULARY ENRICHMENT TABLE   UNIT 4

		my		
		your		
	in	his		
What is		her	_____	?
	on	the		
		this		
		that		

purse	shopping bag	lunch box	clothes closet
package	storage space	wall	roof
can	suitcase	shopping list	
refrigerator	sink	stove	pantry

NO
PARKING

BETWEEN
8 a.m. and 5 p.m.

NO
U
TURN

13

UNIT 5

1.

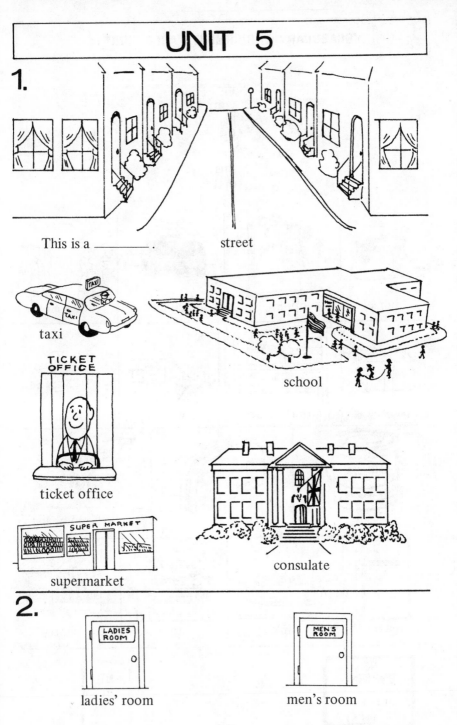

This is a ——————. street

taxi

school

ticket office

consulate

supermarket

2.

ladies' room

men's room

14

3. What is your nationality?

I am _____ .

Mexican   Puerto Rican   Italian

4. Where's _____ ?

Mr. Beck   Mrs. Morris   Mr. Kelly   Mrs. Beck

Mr. Kent   Miss Bennet   Mr. Ben   Mrs. Link

A: Where's Mr. Beck?
B: He's in the restaurant.

A: Where's Mrs. Morris?
B: She's in the bus.

A: Where's Mr. Kelly?
B: He's in the barbershop.

A: Where's Mrs. Beck?
B: She's in the supermarket.

A: Where's Mr. Kent?
B: He's in the ticket office.

A: Where's Miss Bennet?
B: She's in the hospital.

A: Where's Mr. Ben?
B: He's in the station.

A: Where's Mrs. Link?
B: She's in the airport.

5.

To the left.   To the right.

6. Where's the bus stop?
    bus station
    station
    ticket office

Where's the restaurant?
    supermarket
    drugstore
    beauty parlor

7.

Where's her room?
    your car
    the men's room
    Washington Street

Where are your tickets?
    his keys
    her books
    your bags

Where's the Mexican Consulate?
    Spanish
    Portuguese
    Italian

16

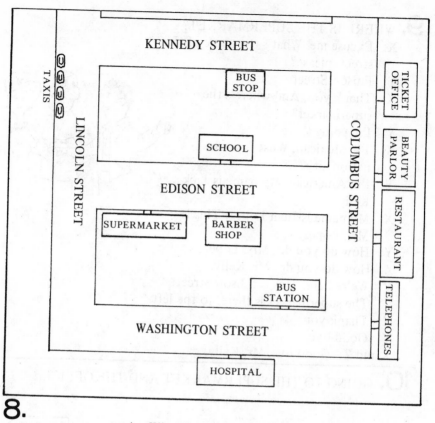

8.

A: Where's the supermarket?
B: It's on Edison Street.

A: Where are the taxis?
B: They're on Lincoln Street.

A: Where's the school?
B: It's on Edison Street.

A: Where's the barbershop?
B: It's on Edison Street.

A: Where's the beauty parlor?
B: It's on Columbus Street.

A: Where's the restaurant?
B: It's on Columbus Street.

A: Where's the hospital?
B: It's on Washington Street.

A: Where's the ticket office?
B: It's on Columbus Street.

A: Where's the bus station?
B: It's on Washington Street.

A: Where are the telephones?
B: They're on Columbus Street.

A: Where's the bus stop?
B: It's on Kennedy Street.

9. WHERE IS THE SUPERMARKET?

X: Excuse me. What's the name of this street, please?

Y: Edison Street.

X: Thank you. And where's the supermarket?

Y: I'm going there.

X: I'm Mexican. What is your nationality?

Y: I'm American. My name is Jack Kelly.

X: My name is Juan Lopez. This is Mrs. Lopez.

Y: How do you do, Mrs. Lopez.

Z: How do you do, Mr. Kelly.

Y: We're here. This is Edison Street. The supermarket is there, to the left.

X: Thank you.

Y: Good-bye.

X and Z: Good-bye, Mr. Kelly.

10. GOING TO THE SUPERMARKET AND THE OFFICE

Mrs. Beck is going to the supermarket. The supermarket is on Edison street. Bus 24 is going there.

Mrs. Beck is going to the bus stop. The bus stop is on Kennedy Street. This is her bus. It's number 24.

Mr. Beck is going to his office. His office is on River Street. He is going there in a taxi.

18

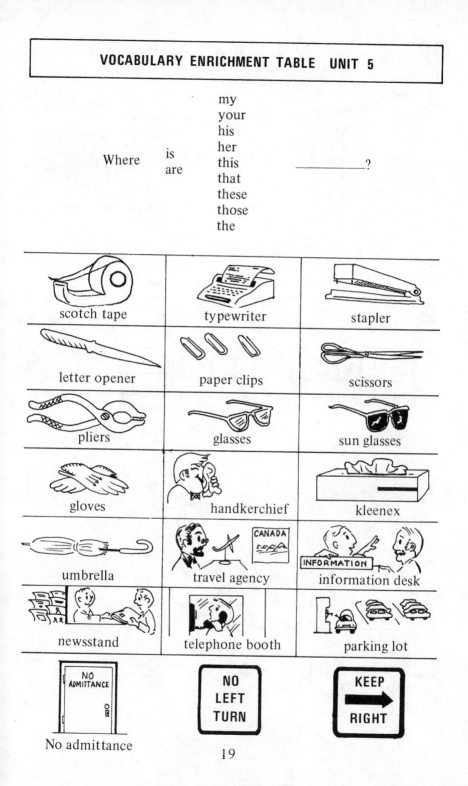

| Where | is
are | my
your
his
her
this
that
these
those
the | _____? |

scotch tape	typewriter	stapler
letter opener	paper clips	scissors
pliers	glasses	sun glasses
gloves	handkerchief	kleenex
umbrella	travel agency	information desk
newsstand	telephone booth	parking lot
No admittance	NO LEFT TURN	KEEP RIGHT

19

UNIT 6

1.

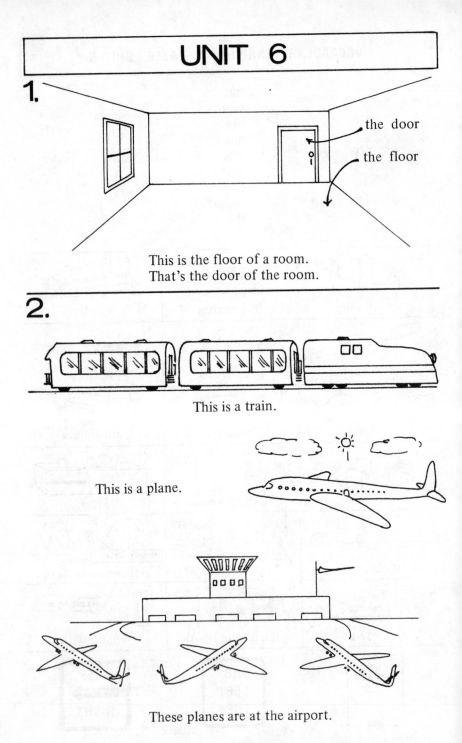

the door

the floor

This is the floor of a room.
That's the door of the room.

2.

This is a train.

This is a plane.

These planes are at the airport.

20

3. Where's the train?

It's at the station.

It's in the station.

4. Where's _____?

the bus

Mrs. Ben

the car

the plane

Miss Kent

Mr. Kent

Mrs. Kent

Mr. Pitt

Mr. Ben

Mrs. Link

Mr. Beck

21

5. AT   ON

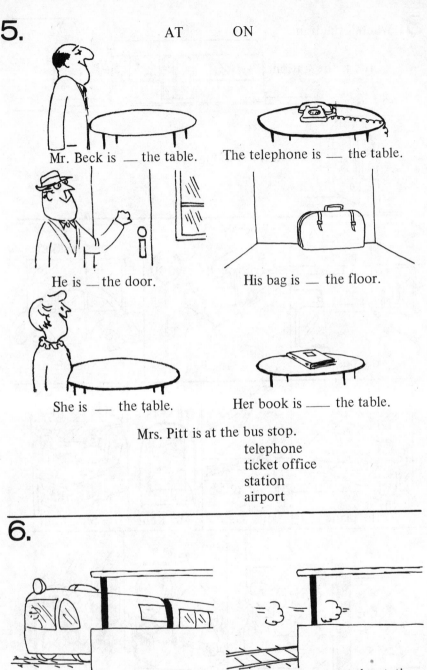

Mr. Beck is — the table.   The telephone is — the table.

He is — the door.   His bag is — the floor.

She is — the table.   Her book is — the table.

Mrs. Pitt is at the bus stop.
telephone
ticket office
station
airport

6.

The train is at the station.   The train was at the station.

7.

Where was	your key?	Where were	your keys?
	his book		his books
	her bag		her bags
	your tickets		your tickets

8.

6 o'clock	12 o'clock	3 o'clock	6 o'clock	9 o'clock
A.M.	noon	P.M.	P.M.	P.M.

morning   noon   afternoon   evening   night

9.

Good morning.

Good afternoon.

Good evening.

Good night.

23

10.

MEALS

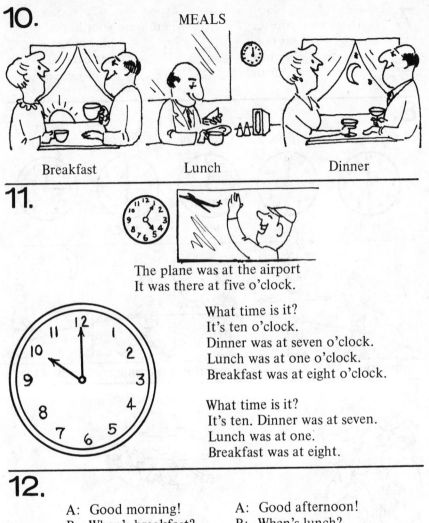

Breakfast   Lunch   Dinner

11.

The plane was at the airport
It was there at five o'clock.

What time is it?
It's ten o'clock.
Dinner was at seven o'clock.
Lunch was at one o'clock.
Breakfast was at eight o'clock.

What time is it?
It's ten. Dinner was at seven.
Lunch was at one.
Breakfast was at eight.

12.

A: Good morning!
B: When's breakfast?
A: It's at eight o'clock.

A: Good afternoon!
B: When's lunch?
C: I'm sorry. It was at twelve noon.

A: Good evening!
B: When's dinner?
A: It's at seven o'clock.

24

13. LUNCH ON THE TRAIN

It's seven o'clock in the morning. Mr. Beck and Mr. Kent are on the train. They are going to California.

X: What time is it, Ted?
Y: It's seven A.M.
X: When's breakfast on this train?
Y: At eight o'clock.
X: And when's lunch?
Y: Lunch is at noon.

It's noon. The train is at the station. Mr. Beck and Mr. Kent are at a table. The seat numbers at that table are twelve and thirteen.

Z: Your names, please.
X: Beck and Kent.
Z: Thank you. I'm sorry, your seat numbers are fourteen and fifteen. These are seat numbers twelve and thirteen.
Y: Where are our seats?
Z: They're there, to the right.
X and Y: Thank you.

14. GOING TO WASHINGTON

Mr. and Mrs. Beck are going to
Washington. They are in a taxi.
The taxi is going to the airport.

It's six o'clock in the evening.
They are at the airport. Mr. Beck
is at the ticket office.

His tickets are in his hand. He
is going to the restaurant. Mrs.
Beck is there. She is at a table.

"When is our plane, Robert?"
"At eight P.M."
"What are our seat numbers?"
"Our seats are 28-A and 28-B."

It's eight P.M. Mr. and Mrs. Beck
were in the restaurant. They are
on the plane. The plane is going
to Washington.

VOCABULARY ENRICHMENT TABLE   UNIT 6

When $^{is}_{was}$ the _____ ?

game

church service

next bus

next train

next plane

last bus

last train

last plane

next show

last show

next city tour

last city tour

parade

race

1.

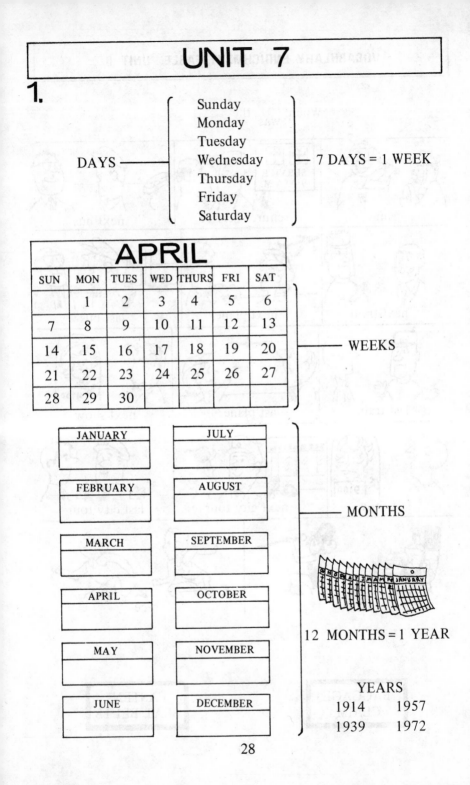

DAYS
- Sunday
- Monday
- Tuesday
- Wednesday
- Thursday
- Friday
- Saturday

7 DAYS = 1 WEEK

APRIL

SUN	MON	TUES	WED	THURS	FRI	SAT
	1	2	3	4	5	6
7	8	9	10	11	12	13
14	15	16	17	18	19	20
21	22	23	24	25	26	27
28	29	30				

WEEKS

JANUARY	JULY
FEBRUARY	AUGUST
MARCH	SEPTEMBER
APRIL	OCTOBER
MAY	NOVEMBER
JUNE	DECEMBER

MONTHS

12 MONTHS = 1 YEAR

YEARS
| 1914 | 1957 |
| 1939 | 1972 |

28

2.

ON	IN
Sunday	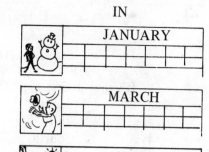 JANUARY
Monday	
Tuesday	
Wednesday	MARCH
Thursday	
Friday	
Saturday	JULY

3.

My birthday is in January.
      It's in January.
           February
           March
           April
           May
           June
           July
           August
           September
           October
           November
           December

4.

DATES

1. It's the	first	1st	of January
2.	second	2nd	
3.	third	3rd	
4.	fourth	4th	
5. It's the	fifth	5th	of January
6.	sixth	6th	
7.	seventh	7th	
8.	eighth	8th	
9. It's the	ninth	9th	of January
10.	tenth	10th	
11.	eleventh	11th	
12.	twelfth	12th	
13. It's the	thirteenth	13th	of January
14.	fourteenth	14th	
15.	fifteenth	15th	
16.	sixteenth	16th	
17. It's the	seventeenth	17th	of January
18.	eighteenth	18th	
19.	nineteenth	19th	
20.	twentieth	20th	
21. It's the	twenty-first	21st	of January
22.	twenty-second	22nd	
23.	twenty-third	23rd	
24.	twenty-fourth	24th	
25. It's the	twenty-fifth	25th	of January
26.	twenty-sixth	26th	
27.	twenty-seventh	27th	
28.	twenty-eighth	28th	
29. It's the	twenty-ninth	29th	of January
30.	thirtieth	30th	
31.	thirty-first	31st	

5.

He was here on   Sunday.
               Monday
               Tuesday
               Wednesday
               Thursday
               Friday
               Saturday

She will be here on   Sunday.
                   Monday
                   Tuesday
                   Wednesday
                   Thursday
                   Friday
                   Saturday

6.

Twenty	20	Eighty	80
Thirty	30	Ninety	90
Forty	40	One hundred	100
Fifty	50	One thousand	1,000
Sixty	60	Two hundred	200
Seventy	70	Two thousand	2,000

7.

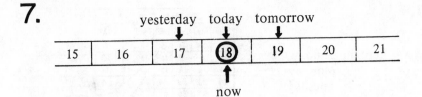

yesterday   today   tomorrow

| 15 | 16 | 17 | ⑱ | 19 | 20 | 21 |

now

Today is the 21st.
Yesterday was the 20th.
Tomorrow will be the 22nd.

Today is the 30th.
Yesterday was the 29th.
Tomorrow will be the 31st.

Today is the 29th.
Yesterday was the 28th.
Tomorrow will be the 30th.

Today is the 28th.
Yesterday was the 27th.
Tomorrow will be the 29th.

Today is the 27th.
Yesterday was the 26th.
Tomorrow will be the 28th.

Today is the 26th.
Yesterday was the 25th.
Tomorrow will be the 27th.

Today is the 25th.
Yesterday was the 24th.
Tomorrow will be the 26th.

Today is the 24th.
Yesterday was the 23rd.
Tomorrow will be the 25th.

Today is the 23rd.
Yesterday was the 22nd.
Tomorrow will be the 24th.

Today is the 22nd.
Yesterday was the 21st.
Tomorrow will be the 23rd.

Today is the 21st.
Yesterday was the 20th.
Tomorrow will be the 22nd.

Today is the 20th.
Yesterday was the 19th.
Tomorrow will be the 21st.

8.

She was here   yesterday.
                at five
                on Monday
                in January

They were there   last night.
                   last week
                   last month
                   last year

She will be here   tomorrow.
                    this Tuesday
                    at ten tonight
                    in September

They will be there   tomorrow.
                      this week
                      this month
                      in 1980

32

9. IN THE HOSPITAL

Mrs. Kent is in the hospital. It is nine in the morning.

Miss Bennet:	Hello, Mrs. Kent, how are you today?
Mrs. Kent:	Fine, thanks. What day is today?
Miss Bennet:	It's Sunday, the twenty-third.
Mrs. Kent:	And I was here last week on Sunday. That's a week. A week in the hospital.
Miss Bennet:	Mr. Kent was here yesterday.
Mrs. Kent:	When was he here?
Miss Bennet:	At eight last evening. His telephone number is on the table. He'll be in his office at ten this morning. And he'll be here at two this afternoon.
Mrs. Kent:	What time is it now?
Miss Bennet:	It's nine A.M. Your breakfast is on the table.
Mrs. Kent:	Breakfast was at eight yesterday.
Miss Bennet:	Today's Sunday. Breakfast is at nine on Sunday.

10. THE BIRTHDAY

Today is March twenty-fifth. Mr. Beck is in his room. A watch, a book and two plane tickets to Mexico are on his table. Mr. Beck is fifty today. It is his fiftieth birthday. His birthday is on Wednesday this year.

Mr. Beck will be in his office at eleven this morning. At ten A.M. he was at the barbershop, and Mrs. Beck was at the beauty parlor.

It's seven P.M. now. Mr. and Mrs. Beck and Bill Pitt are in a Mexican restaurant.
"When's your birthday, Bill?"
"In February, on the twenty-fifth of February."
"That was last month."
"Yes, I was twenty-nine last month."
"I'm fifty today, and Nelly was forty-seven last Sunday."
"Oh, Robert . . . !"
"Sorry, Nelly."

VOCABULARY ENRICHMENT TABLE   UNIT 7

S	M	T	W	Th	F	S

the workdays

the weekend

a holiday weekend: Saturday, Sunday and a holiday on Monday

a day of work

a day of sick leave

a holiday

a vacation at the beach.

What are the holidays in the U. S.? When are they?

New Year's Day		the 1st of January. (Jan. 1)
George Washington's Day		the third Monday in February.
Easter Sunday		a Sunday in March or April.
Memorial Day		the last Monday in May.
Independence Day	is on	the 4th of July. (July 4)
Labor Day		the first Monday in September.
Columbus Day		the second Monday in October.
Veterans' Day		the fourth Monday in October.
Thanksgiving		the fourth Thursday in November.
Christmas		the 25th of December. (Dec. 25)

Fifty-two weeks in a year. Five days of work in a week.
Two weeks of vacation in a year of work.
Five days of sick leave in a year of work.

standard time
last Sunday in October to the last Sunday in April

daylight saving time
last Sunday in April to the last Sunday in October

35

1.

MEN

WOMEN

MAN   WOMAN

Mr. Beck is a man.
He is Mrs. Beck's husband.
He is Tommy's father.
He is Lily's father.
He is Mr. Kent's friend.

HUSBAND and WIFE

Mrs. Beck is a woman.
She is Mr. Beck's wife.
She is Tommy's mother.
She is Lily's mother.
She is Mrs. Kent's friend.

A FAMILY

Mr. and Mrs. Beck
Tommy and Lily Beck

THEIR FRIENDS

Mr. and Mrs. Kent

Mr. Beck is Mr. Kent's friend.
Mrs. Beck is Mrs. Kent's friend.

2.

CHILD   CHILD

BROTHER   SISTER   BOY   CHILDREN   GIRL

Tommy and Lily Beck

Tommy is a boy. He's a child.   Lily is a girl. She's a child.
He is Lily's brother.   She is Tommy's sister.
He is Mr. Beck's son.   She is Mr. Beck's daughter.
He is Mrs. Beck's son.   She is Mrs. Beck's daughter.

Tommy and Lily Beck are children.
And their friends are children.
These are Tommy's and Lily's friends.

3.

Mr. and Mrs. Beck   Mr. Kelly   Mr. and Mrs. Spyros
are married.   is single.   are divorced.
                                      They were married.

4.

A: Is this the supermarket?
B: Yes, it is.
A: Is it White's supermarket?
B: No, it's the Belmont supermarket.

Is this your car?
        ticket
        book
        husband
        wife   Is her father there?
        son   his mother
        daughter   your sister
                37   my brother

5.

Is this the hospital?
No. It's the school.

Is this the bus station?
Yes. It's the bus station.

Is this the restaurant?
No. It's the store.

Is this the store?
No. It's the restaurant.

Is this the school?
No. It's the hospital.

Is this the drugstore?
No. It's the barbershop.

Is this the supermarket?
Yes. It's the supermarket.

Is this the supermarket?
No. It's the Mexican restaurant.

Is this Columbus Street?
No. It's Edison Street.

Is this the bus stop?
Yes. It's the bus stop.

Is this the ticket office?
Yes. It's the ticket office.

Is this the ladies' room?
Yes. It's the ladies' room.

6.

A: Is that Number 7 or Number 1?
B: It's Number 7.

Is that	five or	six?
	two	three
	nine	eight
	seven	ten

7.

He's going to the station on	Sunday.	Is he going there on	Wednesday?
	Monday		Thursday
	Tuesday		Friday
	Wednesday		Saturday

Are they going to the	station?	Yes, they are.
	office	No, they aren't.
	drug store	
	supermarket	

8.

Is the man going to the bus station or to the bus stop?
He's going to the bus stop.

Is the taxi going to the station or to the airport?
It's going to the airport.

Is the woman going to the store or to the supermarket?
She's going to the supermarket.

Is the car going to the station or to the hospital?
It's going to the hospital.

Is Mr. Beck going to his office or to his room?
He's going to his office.

Is Mr. Kent going to the train or to the ticket office?
He's going to the ticket office.

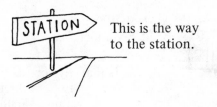

This is the way to the station.

Is this the way to the | airport?
ticket office
barber-shop
supermarket

Is this the way to | Columbia Street?
Central Station
Room 24
Mr. Beck's office

10.

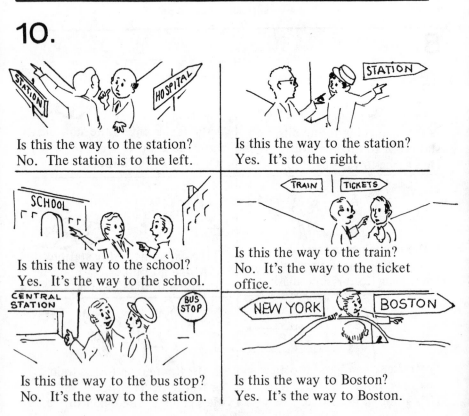

Is this the way to the station?
No. The station is to the left.

Is this the way to the station?
Yes. It's to the right.

Is this the way to the school?
Yes. It's the way to the school.

Is this the way to the train?
No. It's the way to the ticket office.

Is this the way to the bus stop?
No. It's the way to the station.

Is this the way to Boston?
Yes. It's the way to Boston.

11. AT THE CONSULATE

X: What's your name, please?
Y: David Bender.
X: And what's your nationality?
Y: I'm American.
X: Are you married, single or divorced?
Y: I'm married.
X: Is this your wife?
Y: No, she's my daughter.
X: Where's your wife, Mr. Bender?
Y: She's in Mexico.
X: Are your children here or in Mexico?
Y: My daughter's here and my son's in Mexico.
X: And you're going to Mexico?
Y: Yes, we are.
X: Thank you, Mr. Bender.

12. THE TAXI IS HERE

Mrs. Beck is going to California. Her brother Frank and her sister Peggy are there. Frank is in Santa Barbara. He is single. Peggy is in Santa Monica. She is married. Her husband is Mexican.

Today is Friday, the nineteenth of March. Mrs. Beck will be in Santa Barbara tonight. She will be there four days. On Wednesday, the twenty-fourth, she will be in Santa Monica. Peggy, her husband and their children will be at the airport in their car.

"What's the time, Robert?"
"It's two P.M. Your plane is at four P.M. Your taxi will be here at three P.M."
"What's your telephone number in the office, Robert?"
"It's 643-5219."
"Will you be in the office tomorrow?"
"No, Bill and I are going to Nancy's."
"Nancy? Nancy Williams, Ed's daughter?"
"No, she's his sister."
"Oh, yes. Her husband is English."
"Her husband was English. They're divorced now."
"Divorced? Nancy is divorced!"
"It's three, Nelly. Your taxi's here."
"Where are my keys, Robert?"
"Here."
"And my ticket?"
"It's in your hand."
"Oh, yes. Good-bye, Robert."
"Good-bye, Nelly."

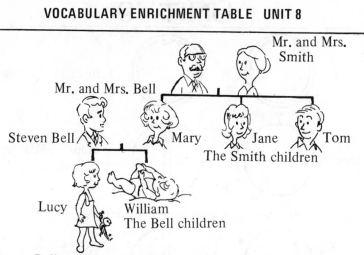

Mr. and Mrs. Smith

Mr. and Mrs. Bell

Steven Bell

Mary   Jane   Tom
The Smith children

Lucy   William
The Bell children

Steven Bell and Mary Smith are married. Mary's father and mother are Steven's father-in-law and mother-in-law. Mary's sister and brother are Steven's sister-in-law and brother-in-law.

Steven is Mr. and Mrs. Smith's son-in-law. Steven and Mary have two children, Lucy and William. William is a baby boy. Mr. and Mrs. Smith are Lucy and William's grandmother and grandfather. Lucy is Mr. and Mrs. Smith's granddaughter. William is their grandson. They have two grandchildren.

Mary's brother is Tom Smith. Tom is Lucy and William's uncle. Mary's sister is Jane Smith. Jane is Lucy and William's aunt. Lucy is Jane and Tom's niece. William is their nephew.

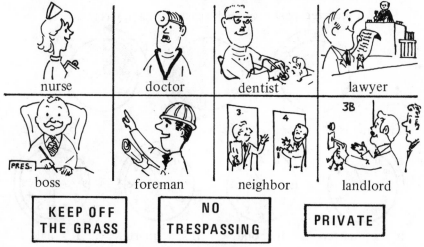

| nurse | doctor | dentist | lawyer |
| boss | foreman | neighbor | landlord |

| KEEP OFF THE GRASS | NO TRESPASSING | PRIVATE |

UNIT · 9

1.

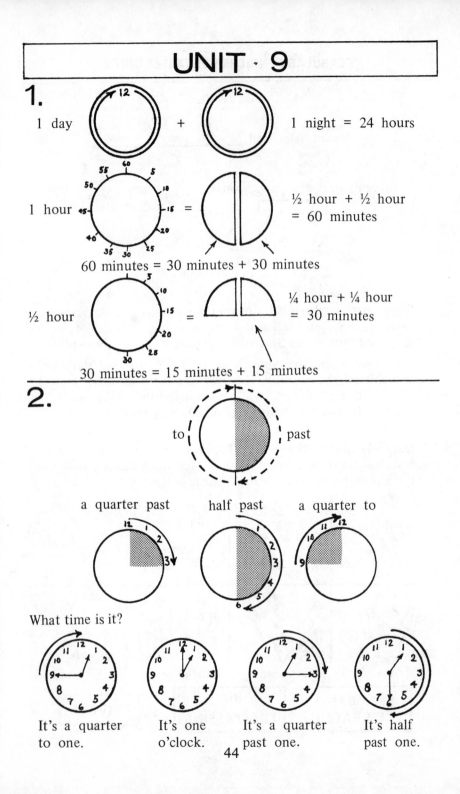

1 day + 1 night = 24 hours

1 hour = ½ hour + ½ hour = 60 minutes

60 minutes = 30 minutes + 30 minutes

½ hour = ¼ hour + ¼ hour = 30 minutes

30 minutes = 15 minutes + 15 minutes

2.

to   past

a quarter past   half past   a quarter to

What time is it?

It's a quarter to one.

It's one o'clock.

It's a quarter past one.

It's half past one.

44

3.

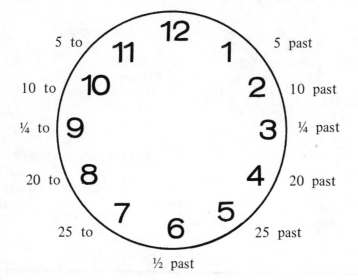

5 to   5 past
10 to   10 past
¼ to   ¼ past
20 to   20 past
25 to   25 past
½ past

What time is it?

It's a quarter past eight.

It's half past eight.

It's a quarter to nine.

It's nine o'clock.

It's ten minutes past nine.

It's twenty minutes past nine.

It's twenty minutes to ten.

It's a quarter to ten.

It's ten o'clock.

45

4. I'm not her brother.
      his father
      his son
      her friend

Breakfast is not at ten o'clock.
      It's not at ten o'clock.
             eleven
             one

I'm not going.
You're
We're
They're
He's
She's
It's

This is not the station.
      bus stop
      ticket office
      airport

I'm not going to the bus.
             train
             airport
             station
             office

The plane is not here.
   taxi
   car
   bus

---

5. IN THE OFFICE

X: Is Mr. Beck here?
Y: No, Mr. Beck is not in his office in the afternoon.
X: When will he be in his office?
Y: Tomorrow at nine o'clock. He's here in the morning.
X: I was here last Thursday at ten o'clock, and he was not here.
Y: Sorry, Mr. Beck was in New York last week.
X: Is he in town today?
Y: No, he is not. He'll be in his office tomorrow morning at nine.
X: Thank you. Good-bye.
Y: Good-bye.

6. WHERE WERE YOU?

Mrs. Beck and her friend Betty will go to the supermarket today. It's a quarter past eight in the morning on a Saturday. Mr. Beck and the children are at the breakfast table.

"Betty's car is here. I'm going now, Robert. See you at Gino's restaurant at twelve-thirty. Good-bye, children."
"Good-bye, Nelly."
"Good-bye, mother."

It's a quarter past twelve. Mr. Beck is on his way to Gino's restaurant.

It's twelve-thirty. He is in the restaurant now. Nelly and Betty are not there.

It's quarter past one. Mr. Beck is going to his car. He is going to the supermarket. Nelly and Betty are not there.

It's quarter to two now. Mr. Beck is going to Gino's restaurant. Nelly and Betty are at the door.

"Hello, Nelly. Hello, Betty. I was here at twelve-thirty. It's ten to two now. Where were you?"
"We're sorry, Robert. We were at the beauty parlor."

47

VOCABULARY ENRICHMENT TABLE   UNIT 9

He	is		this
She	are	not going	that
We		to	my
They	will not go		your

this
that
my
your
his
her
our
their
the

He
She   is
We   are   not going   to   _____ .
They   will not go

night club

insurance agent

bar

laundromat

building

tailor

house

ship

place

night school class

cleaners

motel

photographer

apartment building

YIELD   ONE WAY   SLOW

48

UNIT 10

1.

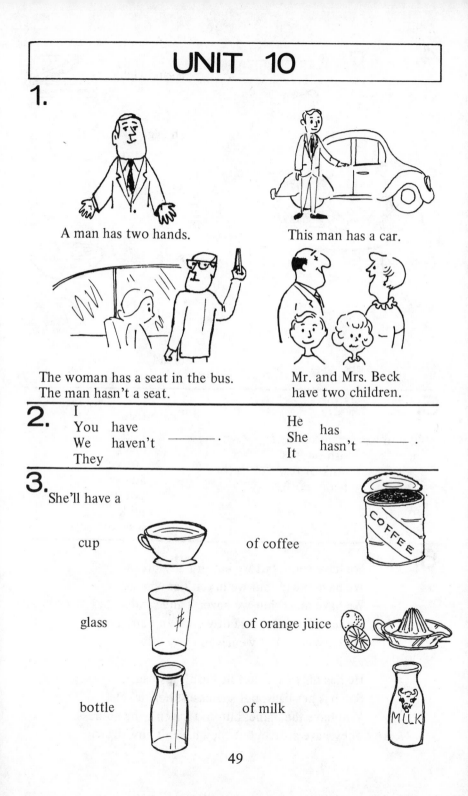

A man has two hands.

This man has a car.

The woman has a seat in the bus.
The man hasn't a seat.

Mr. and Mrs. Beck
have two children.

2.

I			He		
You	have	———.	She	has	———.
We	haven't		It	hasn't	
They					

3.

She'll have a

cup   of coffee

glass   of orange juice

bottle   of milk

49

4.

I'll have _____.

a sandwich

an egg

a potato

soup

meat

bread

5.

Will you have meat or fish?
fish or eggs
milk or tea
tea or coffee

I'll have fish.
soup
meat
coffee
an egg
potatoes
milk
a sandwich

6.

We have soup, but we haven't any bread.
We have bread, but we haven't any meat.
We have meat, but we haven't any sandwiches.
We have sandwiches, but we haven't any eggs.
We have eggs, but we haven't any salt.

He has his ticket, but he hasn't his bag.
She has her bags, but she hasn't her tickets.
You have the name, but you haven't the address.
They have coffee, but they haven't any sugar.

He has coffee, but he hasn't any tea.
      meat   fish
      salt   sugar

They have eggs, but they haven't any sandwiches.
       potatoes   bread
       water   milk

7.

Have you any _____ ?

tea

coffee

water

sugar   salt   fish

Have you any salt?
       sugar
       water
       bread
       sandwiches
       eggs
       potatoes

8.

Have you any children?   Yes, I have.
         sons   No, I haven't.
         daughters
         brothers
         sisters

9. I'LL HAVE MY COFFEE NOW

Mr. Kent's family is at the breakfast table. It's seven-thirty in the morning.

Mr. Kent: I'll have my coffee now, please.
Mrs. Kent: Your coffee's here, Ted, but we haven't any sugar today.
Mr. Kent: Where's the milk?
Mrs. Kent: It's there, on your left.
Mr. Kent: Oh yes, thank you.
Kate: Where's my egg?
Jack: I haven't any salt.
Mrs. Kent: Your egg is here, Kate, and the salt is there, Jack.
Kate: Thank you, mother.
Mr. Kent: It's a quarter to eight. I'm going now. Good-bye, Helen. Good-bye, children.
Kate: Good-bye, father.
Jack: Good-bye, father. See you later.

10. LUNCH IN THE CAR

It's Sunday. Mr. Kent and his family are going to Newtown. They are going there in their car. They have sandwiches in a bag on the seat. They will have their lunch in the car. They will have sandwiches, eggs, bread, coffee and milk.

It's noon now. The family are having their lunch.
"I'll have a sandwich, please."
Jack is having a sandwich, and Mr. Kent is having an egg.
"Where's the salt, Helen?"
"We haven't any salt, Ted. I'm sorry."
"Where's the orange juice, mother?"
"We haven't any orange juice, Jack, but we have milk."
"I'll have my coffee now, Helen. Where's the sugar?"
"We haven't any sugar, Ted."
"We haven't any sugar, we haven't any orange juice, we haven't any salt . . . we'll go to a restaurant."

VOCABULARY ENRICHMENT TABLE   UNIT 10

Have you any _____?   Yes, I have.
No, I haven't.

cigars

pizzas

oil

liquor

chocolate

flour

wine

ice cream

potato chips

beer

fruit

chewing gum

soft drinks

bacon

cookies

Coke

onions

pies

garlic

cake

| CHECK ROOM | REST ROOM | EXIT |

54

UNIT 11

1. Where is he going?

TRAINS

He's going to the train.

supermarket

restaurant

beauty parlor

drugstore

airport

bus station

Where is he going?
Where is she going?
Where is it going?

He's going to _____.
She's going to _____.
It's going to _____.

55

2.

Where are you going?
we
they

Where is he going?
she
it

3.

The train was at the station
at three.

A: When was it at the station?
B: At three.

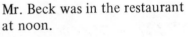

Mr. Beck was in the restaurant
at noon.

A: When _____?
B: At _____ .

This woman was at the beauty
parlor yesterday.

A: When _____?
B: _____ .

Mrs. Kent was in the hospital
last week.

A: When _____?
B: _____ .

4.

Is she going there today?
tomorrow
in December
on Monday

Yes, she is.
No, she isn't.

Are you going to the office today?   Yes, I am.
                    to the station   No, I'm not.
                    to the beauty parlor
                    to the hospital

          When are you going to the supermarket?
                              drugstore
                              ticket office
                              store

5.

When will he be at the station?   When was he at the station?
          at the store   at the store
          at the airport   at the airport
          at the restaurant   at the restaurant
          in his office   in his office

6.

Mr. Bennet will be in his office this afternoon.
A: When will he be in his office?
B: He'll be there this afternoon.

His car will be at the station at five.
A: When will _____ ?
B: It will _____ .

Her husband will be here at six.
A: When _____ ?
B: He _____ .

They'll be here on Monday.
A: When _____?
B: They'll _____ .

Mr. Bennet will be in his
room this evening.
A: When _____?
B: He'll _____ .

7.

He was there yesterday.
Was he there yesterday?   Yes, he was.
When was he there?

He is going there now.
Is he going there now?   Yes, he is.
When is he going there?

He will be there tomorrow.
Will he be there tomorrow?   Yes, he will be.
When will he be there?

8.

Just a minute!
This is your bag.

58

9. ON THE TELEPHONE

X: Hello, is Mr. Beck there?

Y: Yes, just a minute, please.

Z: Hello.

X: Hello, is that you, Robert?

Z: Yes. Hello, Bill. How are you?

X: Fine, thanks, and you?

Z: Fine.

X: Are you going to Bennet's office today?

Z: Yes, I am.

X: When are you going?

Z: I'm going there now.

X: When will you be there?

Z: At ten-thirty.

X: I'll be there at ten. Good-bye.

Z: Good-bye, Bill, see you later.

10. THE PLANE TICKET

Mr. Bennet is at the airport. "Where are you going?"
"To Chicago."
"Your ticket, please."
"Just a minute. It was in my bag."
Mr. Bennet's ticket is not in his bag.

Mr. Bennet is going to the telephone.
"Hello, Robert. This is Mike. I'm at the airport. Is my plane ticket on the table in your office? It was there this morning."
"Sorry, Mike, it isn't here. Just a minute. Mrs. Link, is Mr. Bennet's ticket on your table?"
"Yes, it's here. Mr. Bennet was here this morning."
"It's here, Mike. When is your plane going to Chicago?"
"At ten past one."
"Fine. I'll be there in forty minutes."
"When will you be here?"
"At twenty to one."

Mr. Beck is on his way to the airport in a taxi. Mike's ticket is in his hand.

It's twelve-thirty. The taxi is at the airport now. Mr. Bennet is at the door. Mr. Beck has his ticket.
"Here's your ticket, Mike."
"Thank you, Robert. Good-bye."
"Good-bye, Mike."

Dial	direct. operator. information. the telephone company. the repair service. long distance. the area code. the police. the fire department. the ambulance. the business office.
I'm sorry, it's	busy. out of order. the wrong number.
Please	hang up. hold the line.

I You We They	say think know hear	it's here.
He She	says thinks knows hears	

FOR LOCAL CALLS

1. Listen for dial tone.
2. Deposit dime or two nickels.
3. Dial seven-digit number.

IN CASE
OF FIRE
BREAK
GLASS

UNIT 12

MONEY

1.

one dollar = five dollars

five dollars = ten dollars

ten dollars = twenty dollars

a quarter   a dime   a nickel   a penny

This is a bank.   FIRST BANK

62

2. HOW MUCH

How much are two half dollars?   One dollar.

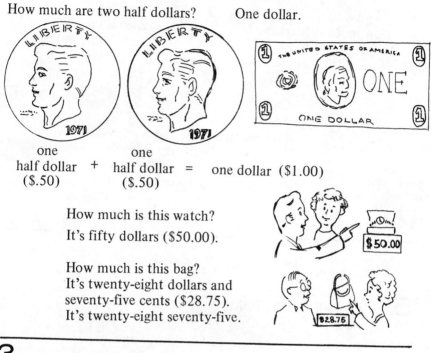

one
half dollar + half dollar = one dollar ($1.00)
($.50)   ($.50)

How much is this watch?
It's fifty dollars ($50.00).

How much is this bag?
It's twenty-eight dollars and
seventy-five cents ($28.75).
It's twenty-eight seventy-five.

3.

One cent ($.01)= a penny.
Five cents ($.05) = a nickel.
Five cents and five cents are ten cents. Ten cents ($.10) = a dime.
   ($.05 + $.05 = $.10) = a dime.
Ten cents and ten cents and five cents are twenty-five cents.
   ($.10 + $.10 + $.05 = $.25) = a quarter.
Twenty-five cents and twenty-five cents are fifty cents.
   ($.25 + $.25 = $.50) = a half dollar.
Fifty cents are a half dollar. Two quarters are a half dollar.
Fifty cents and fifty cents are one dollar ($.50 + $.50 = $1.00).
Two half dollars are one dollar ($.50 + $.50 = $1.00).
One dollar ($1.00).
Two dollars ($2.00).
Five dollars ($5.00).
Ten dollars ($10.00).
Twenty dollars ($20.00).
One dollar and twenty-five cents. One twenty-five ($1.25).
Eight dollars and fifty cents. Eight fifty ($8.50).
Three dollars and sixty-nine cents. Three sixty-nine ($3.69).

63

4.

How much is breakfast?　　　How much is this car?
　　　　lunch　　　　　　　　　　this watch
　　　　dinner　　　　　　　　　　this book
　　　　　　　　　　　　　　　　this room

How much are the eggs?
　　　　　　the potatoes
　　　　　　the sandwiches
　　　　　　the three meals

5.　AT THE BOOKSTORE

X: How much is this book?
Y: Three fifty. ($3.50)
X: Have you any Spanish books?
Y: Yes, they're there, to the left.
X: How much is this book?
Y: Six twenty-five. ($6.25)
X: Have you any Portuguese books?
Y: Sorry, we haven't any Portuguese books.
X: I'll have this book. How much is it?
Y: Two seventy-five, please. ($2.75)

6. ON THE WAY TO THE BANK

It is Friday, the twenty-seventh of January. Mr. Beck is going to Davidson's store. Davidson's store has books, pens, address books and telephone books.
"Hello, Robert, where are you going?"
"Hello, Ted. I'm going to Davidson's store. And where are you going?"
"I'm going to the bank. It's the twenty-seventh and I haven't any money. See you later, Robert."
"Good-bye, Ted."

Mr. Beck is now at Davidson's store. "How much is this pen?"
"Seven dollars." ($7.00)
"And how much is that pen?"
"Fifteen ninety-nine." ($15.99)
"I'll have the seven-dollar pen, please."

Now it's two in the afternoon. Mr. Kent is on his way to the office and Mr. Beck is on his way to the bank.
"Hello, Robert, are you going to the office?"
"No, I'm going to the bank. Where are you going?"
"I'm going to the office. I was at the bank at noon."
"I'll see you at the office, Ted."
"Good-bye, Robert."

VOCABULARY ENRICHMENT TABLE   UNIT 12

Have you $\frac{a}{an}$ _____ ?

Where's your _____ ?

account	checkbook
account number	bankbook
checking account	identification card (I.D. card)
savings account	credit card
check	deposit slip
traveler's check	signature

TELLER	ACCOUNTS	DEPOSITS	LOANS

1.

This is _____ .

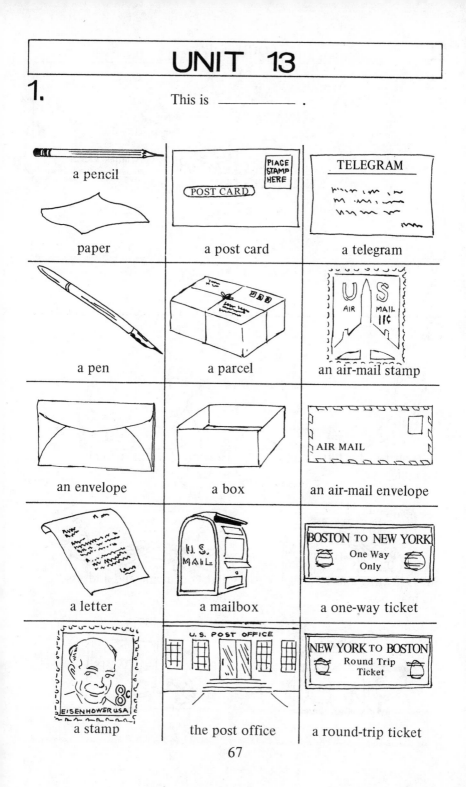

a pencil	a post card	a telegram
paper	a parcel	an air-mail stamp
a pen	a box	an air-mail envelope
an envelope	a mailbox	a one-way ticket
a letter	the post office	a round-trip ticket
a stamp		

67

2.

COUNTRIES

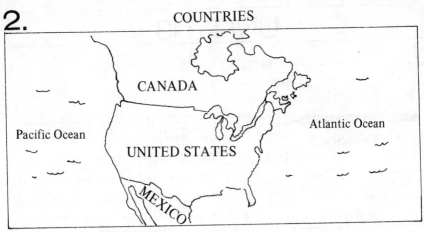

Canada, the U.S.A., and Mexico are countries.

3.

He is putting his letters on the table.

How much is this parcel to Mexico?

She is putting a letter in the mail box.

Put your name and address here.

How much is a post card to Canada?
                              Mexico
                              Puerto Rico
                              Portugal
                              Australia
                              Brazil
                              Italy

How much is this parcel to Holland?
                     this letter
                     this air-mail letter

Put your name here.
             wife's name
             father's name
             address
             room number
             telephone number
             license number
             social security number

Put your bags there.
             pen
             pencils
             keys
             money

1. Put the address on the envelope.
2. Put a stamp on the envelope.
3. Put the letter in the envelope.
4. Put it in the mailbox.

4. MRS. BECK'S LETTER TO HER HUSBAND

1. Mrs. Beck is putting her name on the letter.

2. She is putting the letter in the envelope.

3. She is putting her husband's name on the envelope.

4. She is putting a stamp on the envelope.

5. She is putting the letter in the mailbox.

6. The mailman is putting the letters in the bag.

7. He is putting the bag in the mail truck.

8. The truck is going to the post office.

9. The man is putting the letter in a box.

10. They are putting the letters in bags.

11. They are putting the bags in a mail truck.

5. AT THE POST OFFICE

X: Here's a parcel to San Juan. How much is it?
Y: Just a minute. Is this your address?
X: No, this is my father's address.
Y: Put your address here, please.
X: How much is it?
Y: Three fifty. ($3.50)
X: How much is a post card to Italy?
Y: Ten cents. ($.10) Air mail is fifteen cents. ($.15)
X: And how much is a letter?
Y: Fifteen cents. ($.15) Air mail twenty-one cents. ($.21)
X: Four twenty-one cent air-mail stamps, please.

6. THE POST OFFICE IS CLOSED

Mr. Beck is in his office. His mail is on the table: two post cards, a letter, and a parcel. Mr. Beck has a pen in his hand. "Where's my address book, Mrs. Link?"

"It was on your table this morning, Mr. Beck."

"It's not here now. Have you Mr. Bennet's address?"

"Yes, just a minute. It's 26 Park Street."

"Thank you. Have we any air-mail envelopes?"

"Yes, they're here."

"Thank you, Mrs. Link."

Mr. Beck is putting Mr. Bennet's name and address on the envelope. He has an air-mail envelope, but he hasn't any stamps. "Have we any stamps, Mrs. Link?"

"Sorry, Mr. Beck, we haven't any stamps, but I'm going to the post office in the afternoon. Put your letter on my table."

"Thank you, Mrs. Link."

Mrs. Link is at the post office now, but the post office is closed. It's a quarter past five.

VOCABULARY ENRICHMENT TABLE   UNIT 13

Send it _____ .

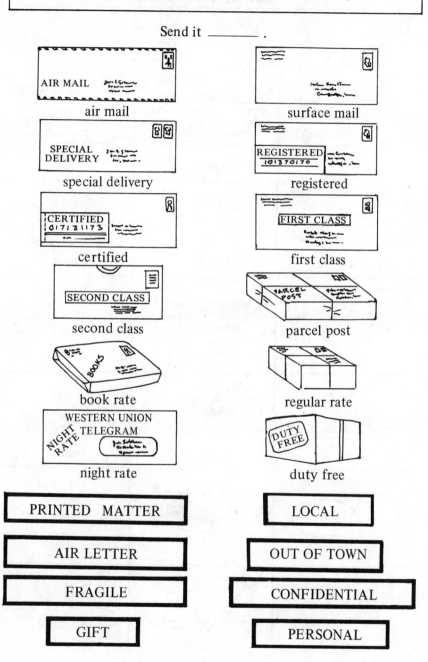

air mail

surface mail

special delivery

registered

certified

first class

second class

parcel post

book rate

regular rate

night rate

duty free

PRINTED MATTER	LOCAL
AIR LETTER	OUT OF TOWN
FRAGILE	CONFIDENTIAL
GIFT	PERSONAL

UNIT 14

1.

Have you any _____ ?

No.
We haven't any _____ .

Yes.
We have some _____ .

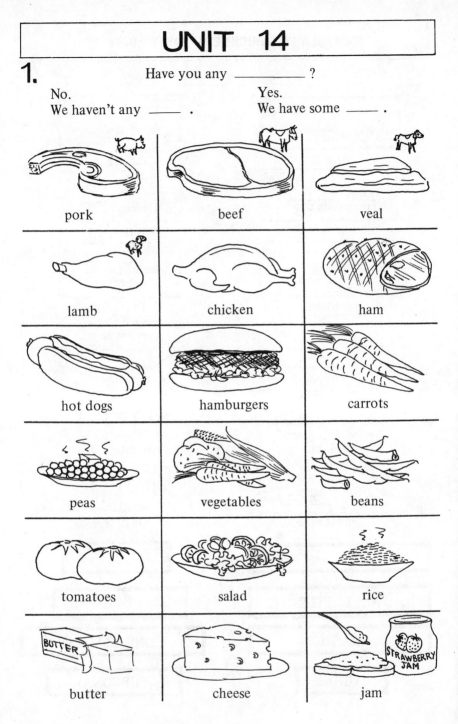

pork	beef	veal
lamb	chicken	ham
hot dogs	hamburgers	carrots
peas	vegetables	beans
tomatoes	salad	rice
butter	cheese	jam

2. This is a menu.

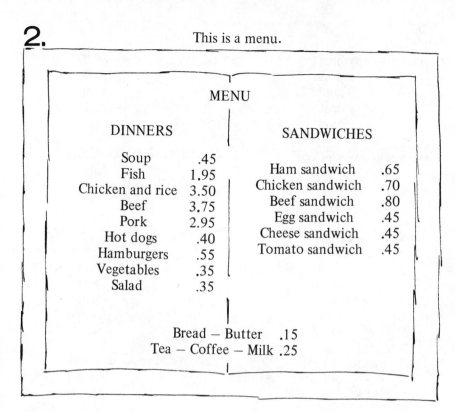

MENU

DINNERS | SANDWICHES

Soup .45
Fish 1.95
Chicken and rice 3.50
Beef 3.75
Pork 2.95
Hot dogs .40
Hamburgers .55
Vegetables .35
Salad .35

Ham sandwich .65
Chicken sandwich .70
Beef sandwich .80
Egg sandwich .45
Cheese sandwich .45
Tomato sandwich .45

Bread — Butter .15
Tea — Coffee — Milk .25

What will you have?

I'll have soup, chicken and rice, and coffee.

This is a bill.

Gino's RESTAURANT

Soup		45
Chicken and rice	3	50
Coffee		25
	$4	20

3.

Have you any beef?
    pork
    lamb
    veal
    ham
	Yes. We have some beef.
	    pork
	    lamb
	    veal
	    ham

Have you any chicken?
    fish
    eggs
    rice
	Yes. We have some chicken.
	    fish
	    eggs
	    rice

Have you any vegetables?
    potatoes
    tomatoes
    peas
    beans
    carrots
    salad
	Yes. We have some vegetables.
	    potatoes
	    tomatoes
	    peas
	    beans
	    carrots
	    salad

Have you any bread?
    butter
    cheese
    jam
	Yes. We have some bread.
	    butter
	    cheese
	    jam

4.

A: What will you have?
B: I'll have fish.
A: We haven't any fish, but we have some meat.

beef	pork
lamb	veal
chicken	eggs

A: What will you have?
B: I'll have carrots.
A: We haven't any carrots, but we have some tomatoes.

potatoes	rice
peas	beans
butter	cheese
coffee	tea

5. HAVING DINNER

Mr. Beck:	"What will you have, Nelly?"
Mrs. Beck:	"What's on the menu today?"
Mr. Beck:	"Beef, pork, lamb, and veal."
Mrs. Beck:	"Any soup?"
Mr. Beck:	"Yes, vegetable soup, tomato soup, and chicken soup."
Mrs. Beck:	"I'll have some chicken soup and beef."
Mr. Beck:	"Any vegetables or salad?"
Mrs. Beck:	"Yes, carrots, peas, and a salad."
Mr. Beck:	"Will you have any potatoes?"
Mrs. Beck:	"No, thanks. I'll have rice. What will you have, Robert?"
Mr. Beck:	"I'll have vegetable soup, lamb, and some peas and carrots."

6. LUNCH AT THE DRUGSTORE

It is Friday noon. Bill and his German girl friend Hildegard are in the car.

"Where are we going, Bill?"

"To the drugstore. We'll have lunch there."

"Lunch in a drugstore? In Germany we have lunch in a restaurant."

"In this country we have lunch in a restaurant, or in a drugstore."

They are in the drugstore now. "What will you have, Hildegard?"

"Have they any sandwiches here?"

"Yes, they have sandwiches and soup. The sandwiches are chicken, ham, beef, egg, cheese, fish, or tomato."

Hildegard will have some tomato soup, a chicken sandwich, and a cup of coffee. Bill will have two cheese sandwiches and a cup of tea.

It's half past one now. They are on their way to the office.

"Are we going to the drugstore tomorrow, Hildegard?"

"Yes."

"O.K. I'll be here at noon."

"See you tomorrow, Bill."

"Good-bye, Hildegard."

VOCABULARY ENRICHMENT TABLE   UNIT 14

I'll have some _____ .

apples	oranges	grapefruit
bananas	grapes	peaches
pears	raisins	nuts
dates	cabbage	lettuce
beets	corn flakes	oatmeal
spaghetti	macaroni	sausages

FRUIT   FROZEN FOOD   MEATS

CANNED FOOD   VEGETABLES   CEREALS

UNIT 15

1.

What's this?
It's pea soup.

Who is that?
It's Mrs. Beck.

What's that?
It's meat.

Who is this?
It's Mr. Beck.

What is it?
It's lamb.

Who is this?
It's Nelly Beck.

2.

Who is going to the _____?
_____ is going to the _____.

U.S. POST OFFICE
Mr. Beck

Mrs. Kent
US MAIL

FIRST BANK
Mrs. Beck

SUPER MARKET
Mr. Bennet

GINO'S RESTAURANT
Miss Bennet

BUS STATION
Mr. Morris

80

3.

The train is coming. The train is going.

Is the train coming? Yes, it is. Is it coming now? Yes, in two minutes.

Is the bus coming? Yes, it is. Is it coming now? No, at two-thirty.

4.

Come in! Have a seat.

5.

Today is Wednesday the 6th. I'm in Chicago. I was in New York on the 2nd. I went to Washington on the 3rd. I went to New Orleans on the 4th. I came here on the 5th. I came here yesterday.

NOW			YESTERDAY	
I	am		I	
you	are		you	
we	are		we	
they	are		they	
		GOING		WENT
he	is		he	
she	is		she	
it	is		it	

81

NOW		YESTERDAY	
I	am	I	
you	are	you	
we	are	we	
they	are	they	
	COMING		CAME
he	is	he	
she	is	she	
it	is	it	

NOW				YESTERDAY	
I	have	I	am	I	
you	have	you	are	you	
we	have	we	are	we	
they	have	they	are	they	
			HAVING		HAD
he	has	he	is	lunch.	he
she	has	she	is		she
it	has	it	is		it

6.

NOW			YESTERDAY	
I	am		I	
you	are		you	
we	are		we	
they	are		they	
		PUTTING		PUT
he	is	it here.	he	it here.
she	is		she	
it	is		it	

7.

Who's going to the post office?	Who went to the post office?
airport	supermarket
store	store
station	station

Who's coming here today?	Who came here yesterday?
tomorrow	last week
on Friday	last month
on the 21st	last year
in June	on Friday
	on the 21st
	in June

Who's having beef?	Who had beef?
pork	pork
chicken	chicken
ham	ham
rice	rice

Who has my pen?	Who had my pen?
my stamps	my stamps
my paper	my paper
my envelopes	my envelopes

8.

I came here yesterday.	I went there yesterday.
You	You
We	We
They	They
He	He
She	She
It	It

9. IN MR. BECK'S OFFICE

Mr. Beck:	Who's there?
Mr. Ben:	It's Richard Ben.
Mr. Beck:	Come in, Richard. Have a seat. How are you?
Mr. Ben:	Fine, thanks. And how are you? How is your family?
Mr. Beck:	Fine, thanks. Nelly and the children are in Newtown.
Mr. Ben:	Is Bill Pitt here?
Mr. Beck:	No, he isn't, but we'll go to his office.
Mr. Ben:	It's a quarter to twelve, Robert. Will he be there now?
Mr. Beck:	Oh, yes. We'll be there in five minutes.
Mr. Ben:	Are we going in a taxi?
Mr. Beck:	No, I have my car. We'll go there in my car.

10. THE TELEGRAM

Mr. Beck's brother Peter is coming to the United States. He is in Germany now. Mr. Beck and his family had a telegram from him today. They will go to the airport tonight. Peter's plane will be at the airport at seven-twenty.

Mr. Beck and his family were at the airport at seven-twenty, but Peter wasn't on the seven-twenty plane. Nelly and the children went to the restaurant. They had some coffee and hot dogs. Mr. Beck went to the ticket office. He came to the restaurant at ten past eight.

"When will Peter's plane be here, Robert?"
"Tomorrow. Tomorrow at seven-twenty."
"Tomorrow?"
"Yes. Here is his telegram: WILL BE IN BOSTON THE TWENTY-NINTH AT SEVEN-TWENTY."
"But we were here at seven-twenty."
"Yes, but today is the twenty-eighth. The twenty-ninth is tomorrow."

I You He She It We They	went to came from	the	town hall city country license office highway patrol immigration office doctor's office clinic dentist optician repair shop shoemaker hardware store	last	year. month. week. Monday. Tuesday. Wednesday. Thursday. Friday. Saturday. Sunday.

Last week Yesterday Last month	I you he she we they	said thought knew heard	it was there.

QUIET

1.

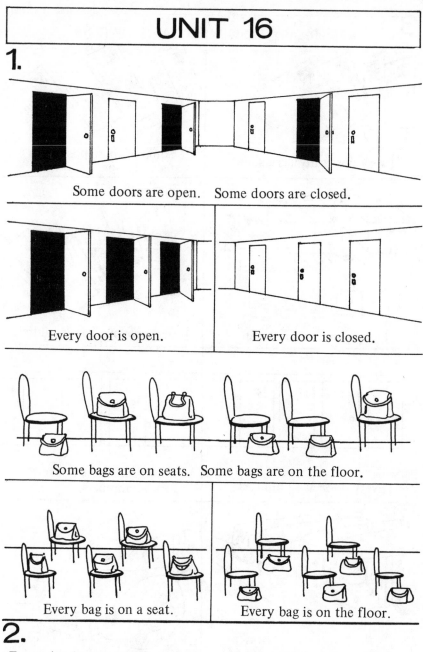

Some doors are open.   Some doors are closed.

Every door is open.   Every door is closed.

Some bags are on seats.   Some bags are on the floor.

Every bag is on a seat.   Every bag is on the floor.

2.

Every day has twenty-four hours.   Every week has seven days.
Every hour has sixty minutes.   Every year has twelve months.
Some months have thirty days. Some months have thirty-one days.

3.

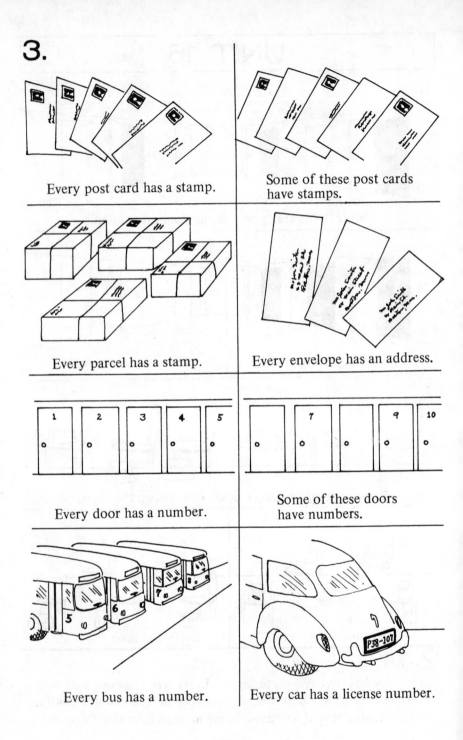

Every post card has a stamp.

Some of these post cards have stamps.

Every parcel has a stamp.

Every envelope has an address.

Every door has a number.

Some of these doors have numbers.

Every bus has a number.

Every car has a license number.

4.

He is having his breakfast now.
And he has his breakfast
every morning.

He is going to his office now.
And he goes to his office
every day.

It is coming here now.
And it comes here every afternoon at three o'clock.

I have breakfast every morning.
You go there every evening.
We come here every afternoon.
They put it there every week.

He
She
It
has breakfast every morning.
goes there every evening.
comes here every afternoon.
puts it there every week.

5.

to the station

from the station

This plane is going from Seattle
to Washington.

This plane is going from New
York to Los Angeles.

6.

Did I have breakfast yesterday?				Yes, you did.			
Did you go there last week?				No, I didn't.			
Did we come here last year?				No, you didn't.			

Did he have breakfast yesterday?   Yes, he did.
Did she go there last week?   No, she didn't.
Did he come here last year?   Yes, he did.

I				I			
You	CAME	here.		you	COME	here?	
We	WENT	there.		we	GO	there?	
They			DID	they			
He	HAD	it.		he	HAVE	it?	
She	PUT ·	it there.		she	PUT	it there?	
It				it			

7.

I have breakfast every morning.   You go there every evening.
Do I have breakfast every morning? Do you go there every evening?

We come here every afternoon.   They put it there every week.
Do we come here every afternoon? Do they put it there every week?

8.

Does he have breakfast every morning?   Yes, he does.
Does he go there every evening?   Yes, he does.
Does it come here every afternoon?   No, it doesn't.

Does this bus go to Boston?
Yes, it does.
Does it go there every day?
No, it doesn't. It goes on Tuesdays.

9.

Do I come here every day?		Does he go there every day?	
you	week	she	month
we	month	it	year
they	year		

10.

We have breakfast every morning.
We don't have breakfast in the afternoon.
Do we have breakfast every morning?
Yes, we do.

She came here yesterday.
She didn't come here today.
Did she come here today?
No, she didn't.

You go there every Monday.
You don't go there on Tuesdays.
Do you go there every Monday?
Yes, I do.

He went there every Sunday.
He didn't go there on Saturdays.
Did he go there every Sunday?
Yes, he did.

It comes here at noon.
It doesn't come here at eleven-thirty.
Does it come here at eleven-thirty?
No, it doesn't.

He had coffee every night.
He didn't have tea every night.
Did he have coffee every night?
Yes, he did.

He goes there every day.
Does he go there every day?
Yes, he does. He goes there every day.

She goes there every day.
Does she go there every day?
Yes, she does. She goes there every day.

11.

Does it go there every day?
afternoon
evening
week
month
year
Tuesday
Friday

Do you go there every day?
afternoon
evening
week
month
year
Tuesday
Friday

Did it go there yesterday?
yesterday morning
yesterday afternoon
yesterday evening
last week
last month
last year
last Tuesday
last Friday

It goes there on Monday and Friday.
Tuesday and Thursday
Saturday and Sunday
Wednesday and Friday

I come here on Monday and Friday.
Tuesday and Thursday
Saturday and Sunday
Wednesday and Friday

12. AT THE STATION

X: Does this train go to Newtown?
Y: No, it goes to Millville.
X: Where's the train to Newtown?
Y: It comes at a quarter to three.
X: When does it go to Newtown?
Y: Every half hour, but on Sundays it goes every two hours.
X: When does the bus go to Newtown?
Y: The bus goes from the bus station every fifteen minutes.
X: Are you going to Newtown?
Y: Yes, I go there every day. Where do you come from?
X: I come from Puerto Rico.
Y: When did you come to this country?
X: I came here in April last year.
Y: This is our train. Good-bye.
X: Good-bye. See you tomorrow.

O'HARE AIRPORT

13. PETER BECK IN CHICAGO

Mr. Beck's brother Peter comes to the United States every two or three years. Last year he didn't come to Boston; he went to San Francisco. His friend Paco was there. Paco is from Mexico. This year Paco is in Chicago. Peter went to Chicago on Saturday.

Peter went to New York and from there his airplane went to Chicago. Paco was at the airport.

"Hello, Peter!"
"Hello, Paco, how are you?"
"Fine, thanks. And how are you?"
"Fine."
"Did you have lunch on the plane?"
"No, but we had sandwiches and coffee."

Peter and Paco went from the airport to town on a bus. From the bus station they went to a Mexican restaurant. They are having lunch there.

"How's your brother's family, Peter? How are Robert
and Nelly and the children?"
"They're fine. They're in Boston now."
"When did they come to the States?"
"In June, last year."

"Did they go to New York?"
"Yes, they went to New York in June, and from there to
Boston. Robert has his office in Boston, but he goes to
New York every month."
"And how are the children? Do they go to school?"
"Yes, they go to school. Tommy is eleven now, and Lily
is nine. How's your family, Paco?"
"Fine, thanks. My mother and my sister Anita are here now."
"Oh, they're here now! When did they come to the States?"
"In April, last year. First they went to my brother Pedro's in
San Francisco. From San Francisco they went to my sister
Carmen's in Philadelphia and from there they came here."

It was five in the afternoon.
"Where are we going tonight, Paco?"
"We'll go to Anita's at six-thirty, and from there we'll go
to Conchita's."
"Who's Conchita?"
"She's my girl friend."

| He She | walks runs rides drives bicycles commutes | to from | the | factory garage gas station snack bar cafeteria coffee shop | every | day. week. month. lunch hour. Monday. Saturday. |

walk

run

ride

drive

bicycle

commute

factory

garage

gas station

snack bar

cafeteria

coffee shop

NEXT EXIT
17 MILES

RAIL ROAD CROSSING

3
TRACKS

UNIT 17

1.

Mr. Ivanov

Mr. Ivanov is
speaking Russian.

Mr. Spyros

Mr. Spyros is
speaking Greek.

Mr. Gómez

Mr. Gómez is
speaking Spanish.

Mr. Fischer

Mr. Fischer is
speaking German.

Mr. Fischer:	Do you speak German?
Mr. Ivanov:	Do you speak Russian?
Mr. Spyros:	Do you speak Greek?
Mr. Gómez:	Do you speak Spanish?

Who speaks Spanish?
            Greek
            Russian
            German

Mr. Gómez speaks Spanish.
      Spyros   Greek
      Ivanov   Russian
      Fischer   German

Mr. Smith doesn't speak Italian.
He doesn't speak Russian.
               Greek
               German
He speaks English.

Mr. Fischer:	Wie geht's?
Mr. Smith:	Sorry, I don't understand.
Mr. Spyros:	τί κάνετε;
Mr. Smith:	Sorry, I don't understand.
Mr. Gómez:	¿Cómo está?
Mr. Smith:	Sorry, I don't understand.
Mr. Ivanov:	KAK BЫ?
Mr. Smith:	Sorry, I don't understand.

96

2.

Do you speak English?	I understand English, but I don't speak it.
Portuguese	Portuguese
Italian	Italian
Spanish	Spanish
German	German

I don't speak English.	I speak Italian.	I don't understand English.
Portuguese	Portuguese	Italian
Italian	German	Greek
Spanish	English	German
German	Spanish	Portuguese

3.

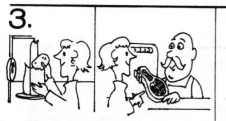

The woman is getting some meat and vegetables at White's supermarket.

She is getting some envelopes at Davidson's store.

She is having some coffee at Kelly's Coffee Cup Restaurant.

She got some meat and vegetables at White's. She got some envelopes at Davidson's. She had some coffee at Kelly's.

We get our	meat	at	White's.	We have	coffee at Kelly's.
	vegetables		White's		tea
	pencils		Davidson's		sandwiches
	paper		Davidson's		

97

4.

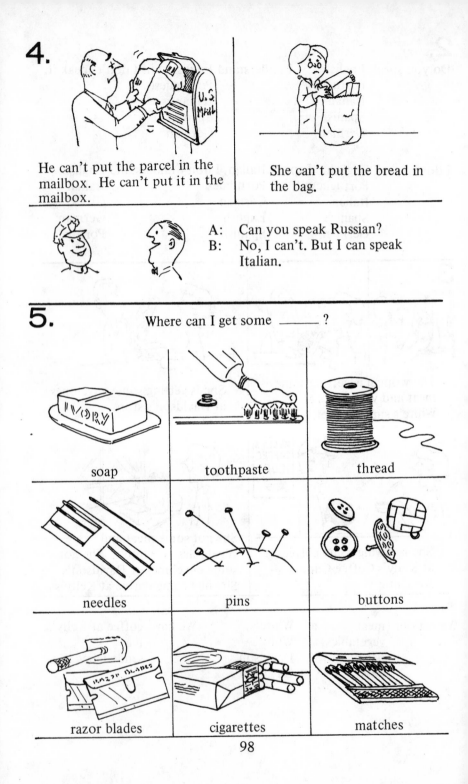

He can't put the parcel in the mailbox. He can't put it in the mailbox.

She can't put the bread in the bag.

A: Can you speak Russian?
B: No, I can't. But I can speak Italian.

5.

Where can I get some _____ ?

soap	toothpaste	thread
needles	pins	buttons
razor blades	cigarettes	matches

6.

Where can I get a _____ ?

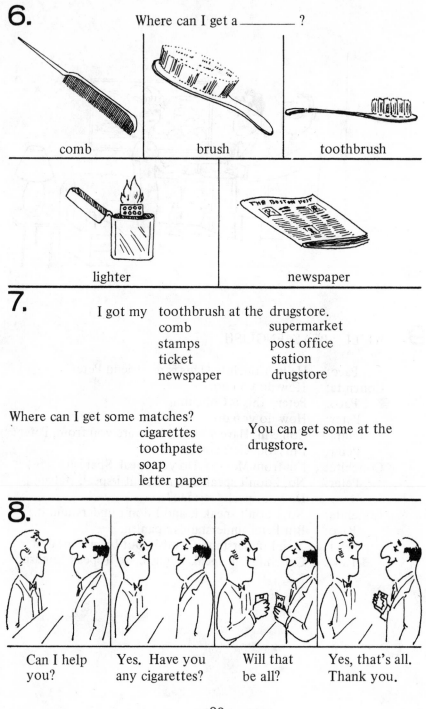

| comb | brush | toothbrush |

| lighter | newspaper |

7.

I got my toothbrush at the drugstore.
          comb   supermarket
          stamps   post office
          ticket   station
          newspaper   drugstore

Where can I get some matches?
               cigarettes   You can get some at the
               toothpaste   drugstore.
               soap
               letter paper

8.

| Can I help you? | Yes. Have you any cigarettes? | Will that be all? | Yes, that's all. Thank you. |

9. WE'LL SPEAK ENGLISH

Paco:	Hello, Conchita. This is my friend Peter.
Conchita:	How do you do.
Paco:	Peter, this is Conchita.
Peter:	How do you do.
Conchita:	Come in. Have a seat. Where are you from, Peter?
Peter:	I'm from Germany.
Conchita:	I'm from Mexico. Do you speak Spanish?
Peter:	No, I don't speak Spanish, but I speak Italian. Do you speak German?
Conchita:	No, I don't speak it and I don't understand it.
Paco:	But Peter understands Spanish.
Peter:	Yes, I understand Spanish, but I can't speak it.
Paco:	Conchita can speak English. We'll speak English.

10. MOTHER'S DAY

It is Sunday afternoon. Peter and Paco are on their way to Paco's mother's. It is Mother's Day today and they are having dinner at Paco's mother's house. Peter has a parcel in his hand. Paco got a Spanish book and some Spanish newspapers at Davidson's. Paco's mother doesn't speak English. She understands it, but she doesn't speak it. She speaks Spanish. She gets her newspapers and her books from Puerto Rico.

Paco's mother is in her room. She got letters and post cards from her friends in Mexico, Italy, and the United States. She got three letters from Mexico City, two from Rome, and one from Los Angeles. She got five post cards from San Francisco, three from Philadelphia, and two from New York. She got a watch from her brother and a pen from her daughter.

It's eight-thirty now. Her friends, her son Paco, her sister Teresa, her brother Carlos and Peter are at the table. They are having a Mexican meal.

VOCABULARY ENRICHMENT TABLE   UNIT 17

Where can I get some _____ ?

cosmetics	nail polish	powder	bobby pins
rollers	shaving cream	adhesive tape	iodine
safety pins	baby food	diapers	hand lotion
aspirin	sleeping pills	pencil leads	ink
ball-point refills	film	flash bulbs	flowers

PRESCRIPTIONS   NO SMOKING

UNIT 18

1.

She wants a match.

She wants an envelope.

He wants a ticket.

She wants a button.

He wants a stamp.

He wants his dinner.

2.

I want a _____.

hat

coat

suit

tie

shirt

skirt

blouse

sweater

dress

3.

I want some _____.

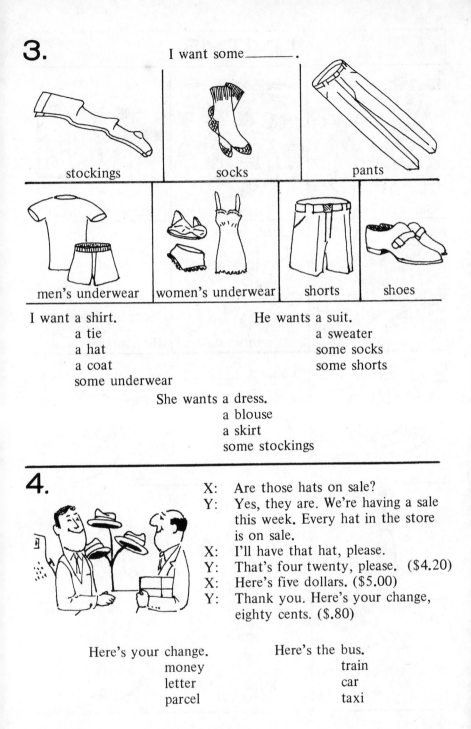

stockings	socks	pants
men's underwear	women's underwear	shorts	shoes

I want a shirt.
    a tie
    a hat
    a coat
    some underwear

He wants a suit.
    a sweater
    some socks
    some shorts

She wants a dress.
    a blouse
    a skirt
    some stockings

4.

X: Are those hats on sale?
Y: Yes, they are. We're having a sale this week. Every hat in the store is on sale.
X: I'll have that hat, please.
Y: That's four twenty, please. ($4.20)
X: Here's five dollars. ($5.00)
Y: Thank you. Here's your change, eighty cents. ($.80)

Here's your change.
    money
    letter
    parcel

Here's the bus.
    train
    car
    taxi

5. I WANT AN ITALIAN TIE

X: Good evening. Can I help you?
Y: Yes. I want a tie. Have you any Italian ties?
X: No, I'm sorry, we don't have any Italian ties.
Y: Where can I get some Italian ties?
X: You can't get any in this town.
Y: Have you any shirts?
X: Yes, here are the shirts.
Y: How much is this shirt?
X: Nine ninety-five. ($9.95)
Y: I'll have it.
X: Will that be all?
Y: Yes, thank you. That's all.
X: That'll be ten forty-five, please. ($10.45)
   Here's your bill of sale.
Y: Here's twenty dollars. ($20.00)
X: Thank you. Here's your change, nine fifty-five. ($9.55)

6. THE SALES

Mr. and Mrs. Beck are in New York City. They want to visit the stores. In January they have sales. Macy's and Barney's are having sales this week. It's eight-thirty in the morning. Mr. Beck wants to go to Barney's first. "You can't go to the stores at half past eight in New York City, Robert. They're closed. They'll be open at nine-thirty."

It's nine-thirty. The stores are open now. Mr. and Mrs. Beck are going to Barney's. Mr. Beck wants a suit, some shirts, and some underwear.
"Can I help you?"
"Yes, I want a suit."
"Here are our suits."
"How much is this suit?"
"A hundred and thirty-five dollars." ($135.00)
"And how much is that suit?"
"A hundred and ten dollars." ($110.00)
"Are these suits on sale?"
"Yes, they are."
"How much is this suit here?"
"Ninety-nine dollars. ($99.00) Do you want it?"
"No, thanks. I'll have the hundred-and-ten-dollar suit."

Mr. Beck got his suit, but he didn't get his shirts and his underwear.
"Do you want some shirts, Robert?"
"Yes, but I haven't any money. My suit cost a hundred and ten dollars! I'll get the shirts tomorrow."
"But Robert, I want a dress and a hat!"
"I'm sorry, Nelly, I haven't any money."
"Can you go to a bank?"
"Not today. It's Saturday. The banks are closed on Saturdays."
"How much money do you have?"
"Twelve dollars. We can have dinner, but that's all."

VOCABULARY ENRICHMENT TABLE   UNIT 18

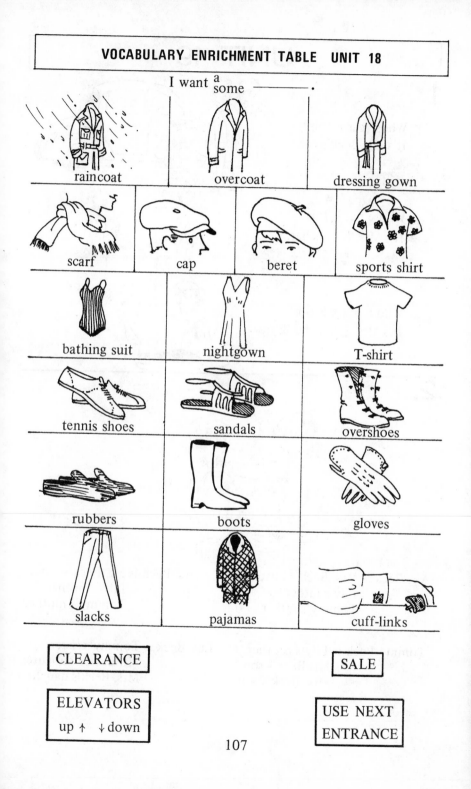

I want a/some _____.

raincoat	overcoat	dressing gown
scarf	cap	beret	sports shirt
bathing suit	nightgown	T-shirt
tennis shoes	sandals	overshoes
rubbers	boots	gloves
slacks	pajamas	cuff-links

CLEARANCE

SALE

ELEVATORS
up ↑   ↓ down

USE NEXT
ENTRANCE

107

UNIT 19

1.

Whose car is this?
It's Mr. Beck's car.

Whose hat is this?
It's Mrs. Beck's hat.

Whose book is this?
It's Mrs. Link's book.

2.

Mr. Beck is Mrs. Beck's husband.
   Lily's father
   Tommy's father

Mrs. Beck is Mr. Beck's wife.
   Lily's mother
   Tommy's mother

Tommy Beck is Lily's brother.
   Mr. Beck's son
   Mrs. Beck's son

Lily Beck is Tommy's sister.
   Mr. Beck's daughter
   Mrs. Beck's daughter

Whose husband is Mr. Beck?   Whose wife is Mrs. Beck?
Whose mother is Mrs. Beck?   Whose father is Mr. Beck?
Whose sister is Lily?   Whose daughter is Lily?
Whose son is Tommy?   Whose brother is Tommy?

Who's Mrs. Beck's husband?   Who's Mr. Beck's wife?
           son   daughter
           daughter   son

Who's Tommy's father?   Who's Lily's father?
           mother   mother
           sister   brother

Whose hat is this?   Whose keys are these?
      coat   cigarettes
      bag   matches
      letter   newspapers

3.

This is a head.

This is hair.

This is an eye.

4.

Milk and salt are white. Some cheese is white.

Butter is yellow. Some cheese is yellow.

Tea and coffee are brown.

Peas are green. Some beans are green.

Meat and tomatoes are red.

Water is blue.

What color is this?
It's black.

What color is this?
It's white.

What color is your coat?
         hat
         bag
         hair

Her eyes are blue.
Her hair is brown.
Her blouse is yellow.
Her skirt is green.
Her hat is red.

His eyes are brown.
His suit is gray.
His tie is blue and gray.
His shirt is white.
His hat is black.

5.

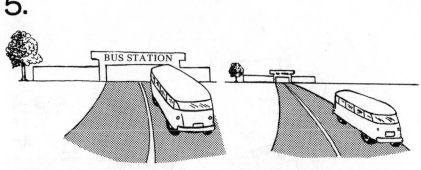

This bus is near the station.　　This bus is far from the station.

The station is near here, but the post office is far from here.
restaurant	airport
store	hospital

6.

DRUG STORE

X: Do you speak English?
Y: Yes, I do. Can I help you?
X: Is the post office far from here?
Y: Yes. It's near the bus station.
X: Thanks. Where can I get some air-mail envelopes?
Y: At the drugstore.
X: Thank you.

7. THE YELLOW HAT

X: Can I help you?

Y: Yes, I want a yellow hat.

X: A yellow hat. . .hm. We have brown hats, black hats, white hats, but we haven't any yellow hats. What color is your coat?

Y: Brown.

X: You can have a green hat, or this blue hat.

Y: A blue hat and a brown coat? No, I don't want it.

X: Here's a French hat, but. . .it's brown.

Y: No, thank you. I have three brown hats. I want a yellow hat.

X: Sorry, that's all we have.

8. SHOPPING IN NEW YORK

This is Mr. and Mrs. Beck's second week in New York. This morning Mrs. Beck and her friend Betty will go to the stores. They will go shopping. Mr. Beck got some money at the bank, but he can't go to the stores today. Today he will visit his friend's office on Madison Avenue. At seven in the evening, he, Nelly, and Betty will have dinner at Alfredo's.

Betty got a brown skirt and a green sweater at Macy's, and some underwear, stockings, and shoes at Gimbel's. Mrs. Beck got a blue dress, a coat, and a blouse, but she didn't get her yellow hat. They went to Andrew's and to Bettina's, but they didn't have any yellow hats.

At a quarter to seven they got a taxi. They put their boxes, their bags, and their parcels on the seat.

Mr. Beck was at the door of the restaurant.
"Hello, Robert."
"Hi, Nelly. Good evening, Betty. Whose boxes and parcels are those?"
"These are my boxes and those green parcels are Betty's."
"What's in this blue box?"
"A hat."
"What color is it?"
"Brown."
"But did you want a brown hat?"
"No, but they didn't have any yellow hats. I got a brown hat...and a yellow coat."

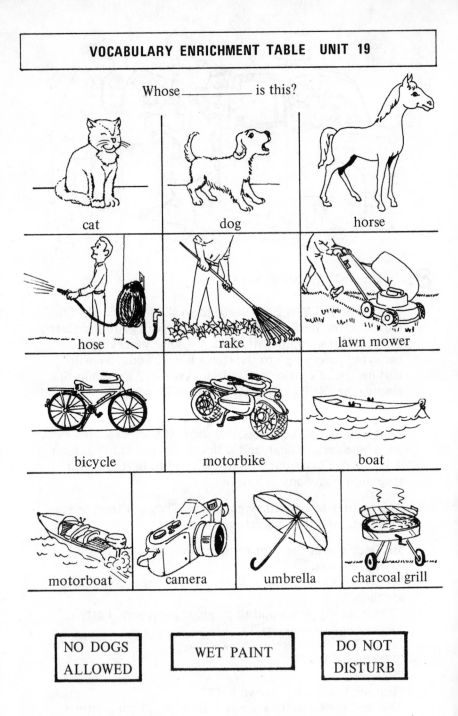

Whose _____ is this?

cat

dog

horse

hose

rake

lawn mower

bicycle

motorbike

boat

motorboat

camera

umbrella

charcoal grill

NO DOGS
ALLOWED

WET PAINT

DO NOT
DISTURB

114

UNIT 20

1.

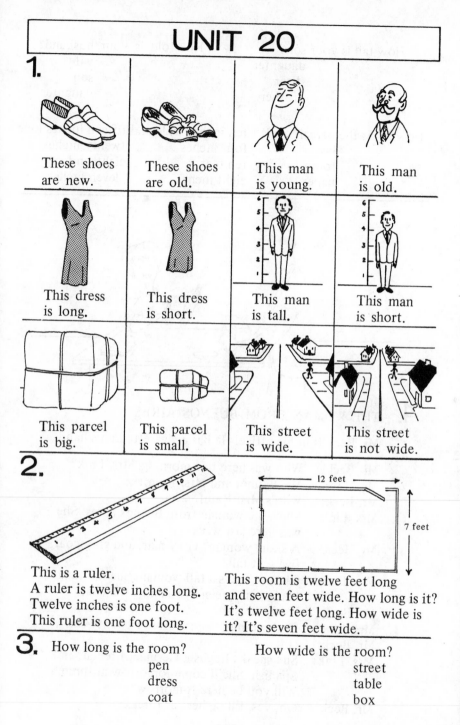

These shoes are new.

These shoes are old.

This man is young.

This man is old.

This dress is long.

This dress is short.

This man is tall.

This man is short.

This parcel is big.

This parcel is small.

This street is wide.

This street is not wide.

2.

This is a ruler.
A ruler is twelve inches long.
Twelve inches is one foot.
This ruler is one foot long.

This room is twelve feet long and seven feet wide. How long is it? It's twelve feet long. How wide is it? It's seven feet wide.

3. How long is the room?
          pen
          dress
          coat

How wide is the room?
          street
          table
          box

115

How tall is your son?	How old is your husband?
daughter	wife
sister	son
brother	daughter

How big is the parcel?	It's ten inches wide and	fifteen inches long.
box	four inches	twenty inches
room	ten feet	eighteen feet
paper	eight inches	eleven inches

4. THE WOMAN FROM BUENOS AIRES

Mr. Beck is in his office. He has a cigarette in his hand.

Mr. Beck:	Who was here this morning, Mrs. Link?
Mrs. Link:	Mr. Bennet and Mrs. Ramírez
Mr. Beck:	Who's Mrs. Ramírez?
Mrs. Link:	She's the woman from Buenos Aires. She was here last week.
Mr. Beck:	A short woman? Gray hair, and gray coat, five feet tall?
Mrs. Link:	Oh, no! She's a tall woman. She has long black hair, green eyes, and a red coat.
Mr. Beck:	How old is she?
Mrs. Link:	She's young; twenty-five or twenty-six.
Mr. Beck:	Oh!
Mrs. Link:	She speaks English, German, French, and Spanish. She'll come tomorrow at three. Will you be here tomorrow?
Mr. Beck:	Oh, yes. I'll be here at three.

5. THE NEW OFFICE

Mr. Beck has a new office. It's on Park Street, not far from the post office. His office is on the third floor. It's a big office, twenty-five feet long and eighteen feet wide. He has a big new table, but his telephone table is old. He'll get a new telephone table at Miller's.

Mr. and Mrs. Beck went to Miller's. Mr. Beck got a small telephone table, twenty-one inches long and thirteen inches wide. Mrs. Beck wants a new table in the kitchen.

"How much is that white table?"
"Sixty-eight ninety-five." ($68.95)
"How long is it?"
"Seventy inches long and twenty-five inches wide."
"That's a big table, Nelly!"
"We want a big white table."
"No, we don't. We have a white table."
"Yes, but it's small and old."
"Do you want this table, Mrs. Beck?"
"Yes, but my husband doesn't want it."

It's two-thirty now. Mrs. Ramírez will be in Mr. Beck's office at three. Mr. Beck has a cigarette in his hand. This is his fourth cigarette in the past half-hour.
"Nelly, it's two-thirty. I'll go to the office now. Mike Bennet is coming there at there."
"Mr. Bennet or that young woman from Buenos Aires?"
"Do you want the kitchen table, Mrs. Beck?"
"No, thanks. We don't want a table."

VOCABULARY ENRICHMENT TABLE   UNIT 20

How | long | is | my your his her their our the | —— ?
| wide | | |

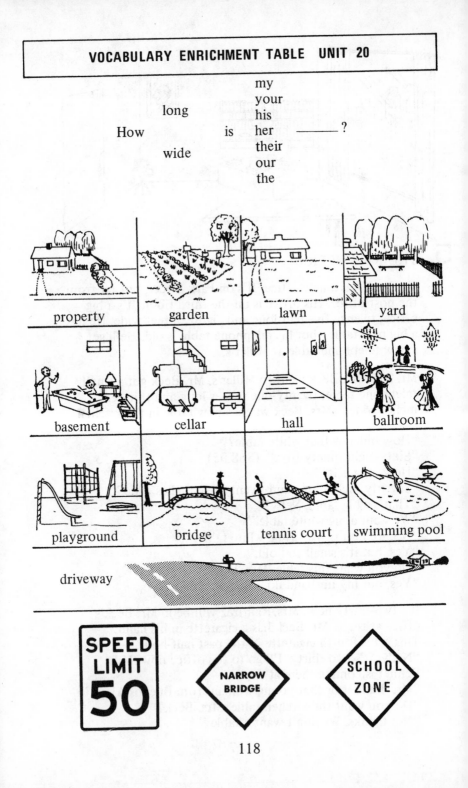

property | garden | lawn | yard

basement | cellar | hall | ballroom

playground | bridge | tennis court | swimming pool

driveway

SPEED LIMIT 50

NARROW BRIDGE

SCHOOL ZONE

118

UNIT 21

1.

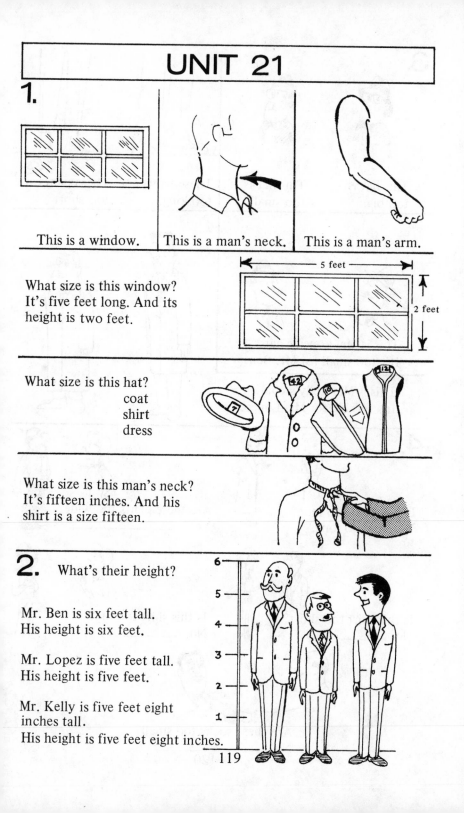

This is a window. | This is a man's neck. | This is a man's arm.

What size is this window?
It's five feet long. And its
height is two feet.

5 feet

2 feet

What size is this hat?
          coat
          shirt
          dress

What size is this man's neck?
It's fifteen inches. And his
shirt is a size fifteen.

2. What's their height?

Mr. Ben is six feet tall.
His height is six feet.

Mr. Lopez is five feet tall.
His height is five feet.

Mr. Kelly is five feet eight
inches tall.
His height is five feet eight inches.

119

3.

This hat is too big.

This hat is too small.

These pants are too long.

These pants are too short.

This is Mr. Lopez's hat. It's too small for Mr. Ben.

This is Mr. Kelly's coat. It's too big for Mr. Lopez.

4.

Is this coat too long?
Yes, it's too long.

Are these pants too wide?
Yes, _____ .

Is this skirt too short?
No, _____ .

Is this shirt too big?
No, _____ .

Are these socks too small?
No, _____ .

120

5.

That sweater is too big for you.   Those shoes are too wide for you
small	long
short	short
long	small

6.

Where's the other shoe? | I want another shirt.
It's near the window? | This shirt is too small.

I have one shoe. Where's the other?
     sock
     stocking

Can I have another sandwich, please?
     hamburger
     cigarette
     match

7.

Mr. Beck is with his family. | Mr. Kent is not with his family.
  | He is here without his family.

Will you have milk with your coffee?
sugar	tea
jam	bread
potatoes	meat

She'll have her tea without milk.
coffee	sugar
bread	butter
meal	soup

121

8. THE RED DRESS

X: Can I help you?

Y: I want a dress, please.

X: What color?

Y: Red.

X: And what size?

Y: Twelve.

X: A red dress, size twelve. Here's a red dress, but it's size fourteen.

Y: Yes, that's too big for me. Have you another in size twelve?

X: No, I'm sorry. We haven't any red dresses in your size.

Y: What size is this dress here?

X: That's a small size. It's a ten. It's too short for you.

Y: Yes, it's not my size.

X: Here's a blue dress in your size. It's forty-nine dollars.

Y: No, that's too much. And I don't want blue. I want a red dress.

X: I'm sorry. That's all we have now. We'll have some new red dresses next week.

Y: Thank you. I'll come next week. Good-bye.

X: Good-bye.

9. THE KENTS GET ANOTHER CAR

Mr. and Mrs. Kent had an old car. It was a small black car.
"When are we getting another car, Ted?"
"Not this year, Helen. We haven't any money for a new car."
"But the old car is too small."
"It isn't too small, Helen. What size do you want?"
"A big car, long and wide."
"How big?"
"Twenty feet long and eight feet wide."
"Oh, Helen, that's too big. That's not a car; that's a bus."

Mr. Kent got a new car, a big blue car six feet wide and
seventeen feet long. They had two cars now: his old
black car and the new blue car. Mr. Kent went to his office
in the new car, and his wife went to the supermarket in the
old car.
"I can't go to the supermarket in this old car, Ted. I want
a new car."
"Another new car! That's too much, Helen."
"But I don't want the old car. It's too small for the
children, the children's friends, the bags from the supermarket. . . and it's seven years old."
Mr. Kent went to his office in the old car, and Helen had
the new car. She went to the supermarket in it with her
friends, to the post office and to the station. In a week
the new car was out of order.
"Ted, do you want the new car?"
"No, thanks."
"Can I have the old car, Ted?"
"Yes, but you have the other car."
"No, it's out of order."
Now Mr. Kent goes to his office in a taxi.

123

VOCABULARY ENRICHMENT TABLE   UNIT 21

What ___ size ___ is ___ the _____ ?
        color   are

carpet | sofa | cupboard

tablecloth | rug | blankets

sheets | bedspread | towels | curtains

drapes | shelves | mirror | washbowl

dishwasher | washing machine | porch | balcony

LOW CLEARANCE 12 FT 6 IN

SMALL | LARGE

MEDIUM | EXTRA LARGE

124

UNIT 22

1.

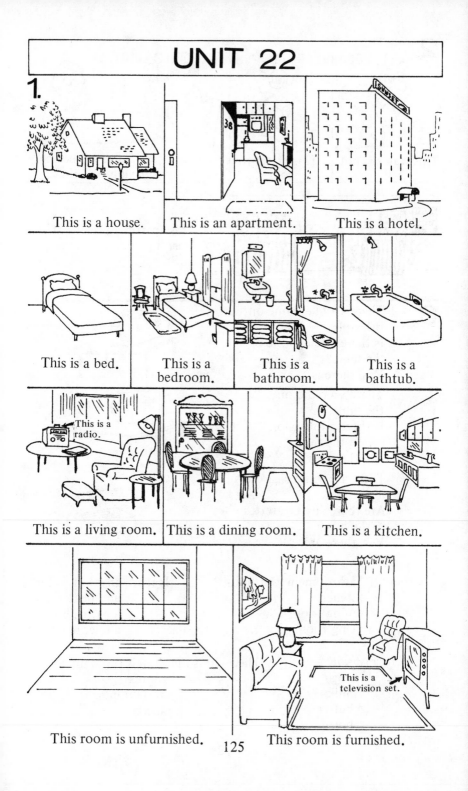

This is a house.

This is an apartment.

This is a hotel.

This is a bed.

This is a bedroom.

This is a bathroom.

This is a bathtub.

This is a radio.

This is a living room.

This is a dining room.

This is a kitchen.

This room is unfurnished.

This is a television set.

This room is furnished.

2.

| This water is hot. | This water is cold. | Mr. Beck is having hot coffee. Tommy is having cold milk. |

This apartment has heat.
It isn't cold.

3.

There's a telephone on the table.
Is there a telephone on the table?
Yes, there is.

There's a radio on the table.
Is there a television set on the table?
No, there isn't.

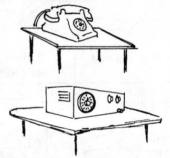

There are some cigarettes in the box.
Are there any cigarettes in the box?
Yes, there are.

Is there a bathroom in the house?	Is there any hot water?
kitchen	any heat
dining room	a bathtub
living room	a telephone

Is there any salt?	There are some hotels on Main Street.
sugar	stores
milk	restaurants
butter	banks
bread	

126

4.

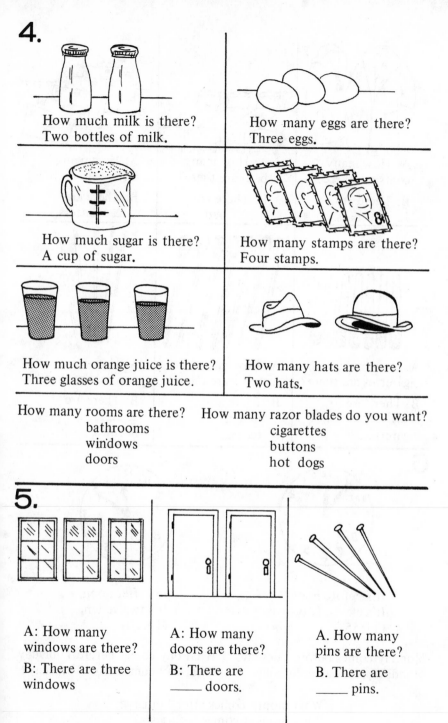

How much milk is there?
Two bottles of milk.

How many eggs are there?
Three eggs.

How much sugar is there?
A cup of sugar.

How many stamps are there?
Four stamps.

How much orange juice is there?
Three glasses of orange juice.

How many hats are there?
Two hats.

How many rooms are there?   How many razor blades do you want?
    bathrooms   cigarettes
    windows   buttons
    doors   hot dogs

5.

A: How many
windows are there?

B: There are three
windows

A: How many
doors are there?

B: There are
_____ doors.

A. How many
pins are there?

B. There are
_____ pins.

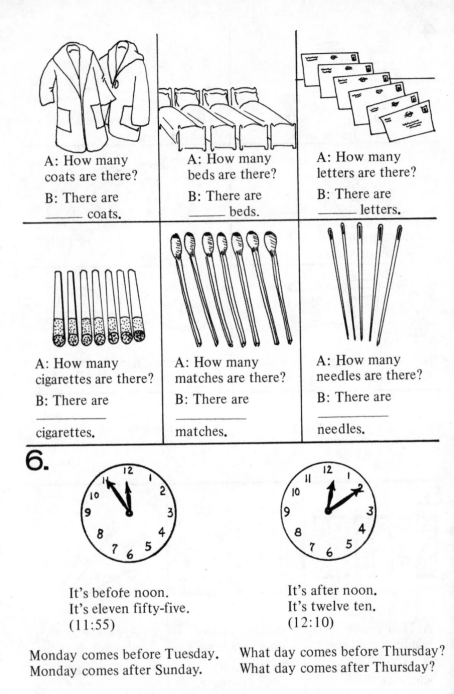

A: How many coats are there?

B: There are _____ coats.

A: How many beds are there?

B: There are _____ beds.

A: How many letters are there?

B: There are _____ letters.

A: How many cigarettes are there?

B: There are _____ cigarettes.

A: How many matches are there?

B: There are _____ matches.

A: How many needles are there?

B: There are _____ needles.

6.

It's befofe noon.
It's eleven fifty-five.
(11:55)

It's after noon.
It's twelve ten.
(12:10)

Monday comes before Tuesday.
Monday comes after Sunday.

What day comes before Thursday?
What day comes after Thursday?

What month comes after January?
What number comes before six?

128

7.

When can we go to the station?   When can I have the apartment?
          airport   the room
          post office   my breakfast
          hospital   my lunch

X: Do you have any furnished apartments?
Y: Yes, there's a four-room apartment on the second floor.
X: How much is the rent?
Y: One hundred and fifty a month, with heat.
X: Is there any lease?
Y: Yes, there is.
X: For how long?
Y: For a year.
X: When can I have the apartment?
Y: You can have it on the first of August.

8.

ON	OFF
The hot water is on.	The cold water is off.

This light is on.	This light is off.	The television set is on.	The television set is off.

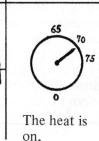

The radio is on.	The radio is off.	The heat is on.	The heat is off.

9. I WANT AN APARTMENT

X: Do you want a house or an apartment?
Y: I want an apartment.
X: For how long?
Y: For six months, October to March.
X: Furnished or unfurnished?
Y: Furnished.
X: There's an apartment on Maple Street. It's a small apartment on the first floor.
Y: How many rooms are there?
X: A living room, a bedroom, a bathroom, and a kitchen.
Y: Is there any heat?
X: Oh, yes, there's heat. The heat will be fifteen dollars a month for October to March.
Y: How much is the rent?
X: It's one hundred forty a month. ($140.00)
Y: And is there a lease?
X: No, there isn't any lease.
Y: Is there a telephone?
X: Yes, there is a telephone in the living room.
Y: When can I have the apartment?
X: On October first.

10. THE NEW APARTMENT

Mr. Beck and his family have a new apartment on River Street. It's a big apartment on the second floor of an old house. There are six rooms and a bathroom and a big kitchen. The living room is twenty feet long and twelve feet wide. Mr. and Mrs. Beck's bedroom has three windows and two doors. There is another big bedroom for the children and another bedroom for Mr. and Mrs. Beck's friends. The bathroom is small, but it has a big bathtub with hot and cold water. There's a dining room and a small room near the kitchen for old dresses, coats, shoes, hats, and boxes.

There are telephones in the living room and in the kitchen. There is a television set in the living room and a radio in the kitchen. There is a long white table near the window in the kitchen.

The children's room is blue. The dining room is gray and the living room is green. The kitchen and the bathroom are white.

The apartment is in a house not far from Mr. Beck's office, and there's a bus stop near the door.

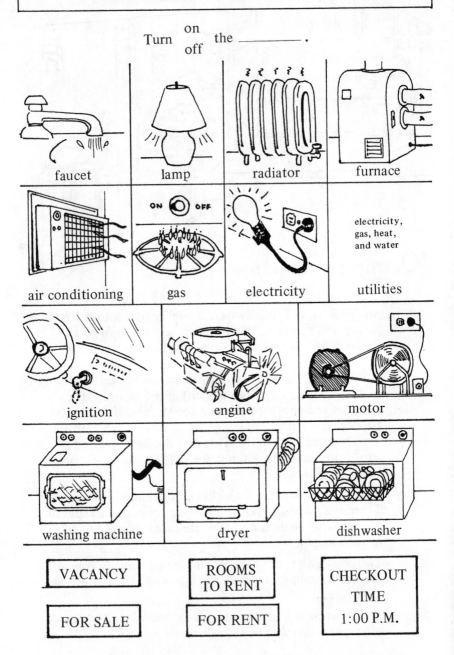

Turn on/off the _____.

faucet

lamp

radiator

furnace

air conditioning

gas

electricity

electricity, gas, heat, and water

utilities

ignition

engine

motor

washing machine

dryer

dishwasher

VACANCY

FOR SALE

ROOMS TO RENT

FOR RENT

CHECKOUT TIME 1:00 P.M.

UNIT 23

1. I am a _____ .

mechanic

driver

repairman

barber

factory worker

farm worker

waiter

waitress

office worker

manager

businessman

secretary

nurse

baby sitter

2. This is a gas station.

This is a garage.

This is a factory.

This is a farm.

133

3.

A factory worker works in a factory.
A farm worker works on a farm.
An office worker works in an office.
A driver works in a car, a taxi, or a bus.
A waiter works in a restaurant.
A secretary works in an office.
A nurse works in a hospital.
A baby sitter works in a family with children.

4.

This man is working in a T .V. store.
He has a job in a T. V. store.
He is a T. V. repairman.

This man is working in a restaurant.
He has a job in a restaurant.
He is a waiter.

This man is working in a barbershop.
He has a job in a barbershop
He is a barber.

This woman is working in a hospital.
She has a job in a hospital.
She is a nurse.

5.

Mr. Spyros	Miss Bennet	Mr. Kelly
Mr. Ivanov	Mrs. Morris	Mr. Ben
Mrs. Link	Mr. Lopez	Mr. Pitt

A: Has Mr. Spyros a job?
B: Yes. He works in a garage. He's a mechanic.

A: Has Miss Bennet a job?
B: Yes. She works in a hospital. She's a nurse.

6.

A farm worker gets $300.00 a month.
His wages are $300.00 a month. He gets his wages every day or every week.
An office worker gets $80.00 a week.
His salary is $80.00 a week. He gets $160.00 every two weeks.
A factory worker gets $2.75 an hour.
His wages are $2.75 an hour. He gets his wages every Friday.

7.

Mr. Spyros is a mechanic. He goes to work at eight in the morning. He works from eight to six. At twelve he has an hour for his lunch. That's his lunch hour.

135

Mr. Ben is a waiter. He goes to his work at eleven. He works from eleven to three and from four to nine. At three he has an hour for his lunch. That's his lunch hour.

Mr. Pitt is a factory worker. He goes to his work at eight. He works from eight to five. At one he has his lunch hour. The factory is closed for two weeks in August, and that is his vacation.

Mrs. Link is a secretary. She goes to work at nine in the morning. She works from nine to five. She has a cup of coffee at eleven, and a cup of tea at four. Her lunch hour is at twelve. She doesn't work on Saturdays, Sundays, or holidays.

Miss Bennet is a nurse. She goes to her work at seven in the morning. She works from seven to four in the afternoon. At eleven-thirty she has forty minutes for her lunch. She works on Sundays and holidays, but she gets three weeks of vacation a year.

8.

What can you do?	I can _____.
What's your job?	I'm a _____.
What time do you go to work?	I go to work at _____ .
When's your lunch hour?	It's from ___ to ___ .
How many holidays do you get?	I get _____ holidays.

136

Do you work on Saturday? I _____ on Saturday.
How many hours a day do you work? I work _____ hours a day.
How many hours a week do you work? I work _____ hours a week.
How much vacation do you get? I get _____ every year.
When do you get your vacation? I get my vacation in _____ .

9. PACO IS GETTING A JOB

1.
Paco wants a job.
He goes to a factory.

2.
Paco: I'm a mechanic. Is
   the manager here today?
Secretary: Yes, he's in his office.

3.
Manager: Come in.

4.
Paco: Good morning. My name
   is Paco García.
Manager: Have a seat, Mr. García.

137

5.
Paco: I want some work.
Manager: What can you do?

6.
Paco: I'm a mechanic. I had a mechanic's job in Mexico.
Manager: For how long?

7.
Paco: For three years.
Manager: I have a job for you.

8.
Paco: What are the wages?

9.
Manager: $125.00 a week, with two weeks of vacation a year. We work from eight to four-thirty.

10.
Paco: I'll be here tomorrow at eight.

10. I WANT A JOB

X: Good morning. My name is Manuel Gómez.
Y: Please have a seat, Mr. Gómez.
X: Thank you. I want a job.
Y: What can you do?
X: I'm a television repairman.
Y: I have a job for a television repairman.
X: What's the salary?
Y: A hundred and twenty a week. ($120.00)
X: Do I work on Saturdays?
Y: No, not on Saturdays. Mondays to Fridays, 8 to 5. Do you want the job?
X: Yes, I do.
Y: Can you come tomorrow at eight?
X: Yes, I'll be here at eight. Thank you.
Y: Just a minute. Please give me your address, telephone number, and social security number.
X: My address is 76 Washington Street. My telephone number is 862-3107. And my social security number is 863-02-9951.
Y: Are you married, Mr. Gómez?
X: Yes, and I have two children.
Y: Thank you Mr. Gómez. I'll see you at eight tomorrow.
X: I'll be here. Good-bye.
Y: Good-bye.

11. TWO JOBS

Paco's friend Manuel comes from Puerto Rico. He came to this country last year. He got a job in a hotel in Sarasota, Florida. He was there from December to May. His salary was eighty dollars ($80.00) a week. In June, July, and August the hotel was closed.

In July Manuel went to the state of Maine. He got a job in a gas station in Brunswick. He works from nine in the morning to five in the afternoon. He has his lunch hour from one to two. He doesn't work on Wednesday or on Friday afternoon, but he works on Saturday and on Sunday evening. The gas station is closed on Sunday morning.

Manuel's family came to Brunswick in July. His wife got a job in a hospital. She is a nurse. She works from seven in the morning to four in the afternoon. On Monday and Thursday she works from eleven in the evening to eight in the morning. She works on Saturday morning, but she doesn't work on Sunday.

I'd like a job as a _____ .
I can work as a _____ .
I've been a _____ .

bookkeeper	draftsman
bricklayer	clerk
carpenter	typist
gardener	night watchman
electrician	dishwasher
housewife	window washer
farmer	painter
builder	dietician
sailor	sanitary worker
tailor	policeman
plumber	librarian
airline worker	lifeguard
teacher	architect
medical aide	engineer
programmer	

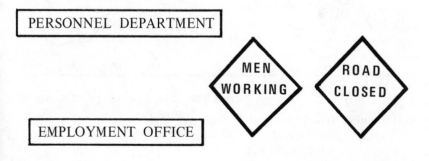

PERSONNEL DEPARTMENT

MEN WORKING

ROAD CLOSED

EMPLOYMENT OFFICE

UNIT 24

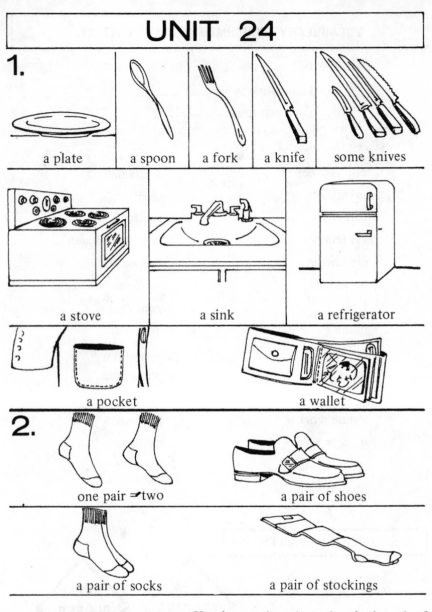

1.

a plate | a spoon | a fork | a knife | some knives

a stove | a sink | a refrigerator

a pocket | a wallet

2.

one pair ⇒ two | a pair of shoes

a pair of socks | a pair of stockings

I want a pair of red shoes.
             brown socks
             white stockings
             gray pants
             green shorts

Here's one shoe, but where's the other?
    sock
    stocking

3.

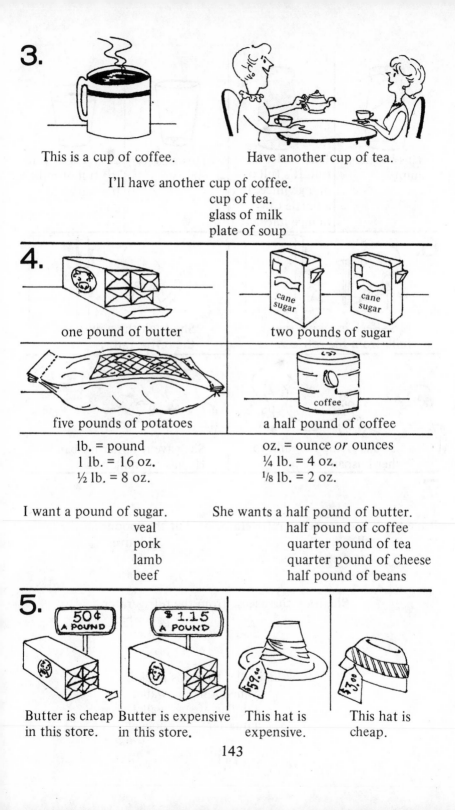

This is a cup of coffee.   Have another cup of tea.

I'll have another cup of coffee.
　　　　　　　　 cup of tea.
　　　　　　　　 glass of milk
　　　　　　　　 plate of soup

4.

one pound of butter   two pounds of sugar

five pounds of potatoes   a half pound of coffee

lb. = pound   oz. = ounce *or* ounces
1 lb. = 16 oz.   ¼ lb. = 4 oz.
½ lb. = 8 oz.   ⅛ lb. = 2 oz.

I want a pound of sugar.   She wants a half pound of butter.
　　　　　 veal   　　　　　　half pound of coffee
　　　　　 pork   　　　　　　quarter pound of tea
　　　　　 lamb   　　　　　　quarter pound of cheese
　　　　　 beef   　　　　　　half pound of beans

5.

50¢ A POUND $1.15 A POUND

Butter is cheap   Butter is expensive   This hat is   This hat is
in this store.   in this store.   expensive.   cheap.

143

This bottle is empty.

This bottle is full. It's full of orange juice. It's a bottle of orange juice.

This glass is empty.

This glass is full. It's full of milk. It's a glass of milk.

6.

Mrs. Beck is taking the milk from the refrigerator.

She took the milk from the refrigerator.

She is giving the milk to her husband.

She gave it to her husband. He has the milk now.

7.

Take the butter from the refrigerator.
     milk
     cheese
     eggs

Put the spoons on the table.
     knives
     forks
     plates

She took the cheese from the refrigerator.
     paper bag
     stove
     box

He took his wallet from his pocket.
     some money   wallet
     a dollar   wallet
     a quarter   pocket

144

8.

He took a newspaper from the table.
He gave it to me.

you	I took the matches from my pocket.
him	I gave them to Mrs. Beck.
her	her
us	him
them	you

9. AT BREAKFAST WITH THE BECKS

Mr. Beck: Can I have another cup of coffee, Nelly?

Tommy: Can I have a glass of milk, please?

Mrs. Beck: Just a minute, Tommy. Here's your coffee, Robert. Tommy, there's some milk in the refrigerator.

Lily: Who took my spoon?

Mrs. Beck: You can get another spoon, Lily.

Mr. Beck: There isn't any butter on the table.

Mrs. Beck: I'm sorry, there isn't any butter in the house. I'll get a pound today. Here's some jam.

Lily: Who took my orange juice?

Mrs. Beck: Tommy, did you take Lily's orange juice?

Tommy: No, this is my orange juice. You gave it to me, Mother. But I'll give some to Lily.

Mrs. Beck: Robert, can I have a cigarette, please?

Mr. Beck: Aren't you having any breakfast, Nelly?

Mrs. Beck: No, I'll have my breakfast later.

10. GETTING DINNER

Mrs. Beck and her friend Betty are in the kitchen of the new apartment. Mrs. Beck has a white kitchen with a big refrigerator, a new table, and a stove. Betty, the Robinsons, and Robert's friend Bill Pitt will have dinner with the Beck's tonight. Betty will go to the supermarket. Mrs. Beck can't go. Her stove is out of order and a repairman will be there at nine in the morning. Betty will go to the supermarket after breakfast.

"How much meat do you want for tonight, Nelly?"
"Two small chickens for the soup and three pounds of veal. And two pounds of beef for tomorrow."

Mrs. Beck gave twenty-five dollars to Betty. Betty took the money, put it in her bag and went to the supermarket. She got the meat there.

It's six in the evening. Mrs. Beck is putting the plates on the table.

"Did you take the potatoes off the stove?"
"Yes, I put them on a plate."
"Where's the soup?"
"It's on the stove."

Mrs. Beck and Betty put the knives, the forks, the spoons, the glasses and the cups on the table. Betty took the veal from the refrigerator. They will have chicken soup and veal for dinner with potatoes and vegetables.

It's six-thirty. Bill and the Robinsons are at the door. "Hello, Nelly. Hello, Betty."
"Hello, how are you? Come in. Have a seat."
"Where's Robert?"
"He'll be here in a minute."

It is seven now. Mr. and Mrs. Beck, Betty, the Robinsons, and Bill are in the dining room. Dinner is on the table.

Where do you keep the _____ ?

pots	frying pans	dishes	kettle
strainer	can opener	bottle opener	carving knife
paring knife	chopping board	rolling pin	baking pans
dish towels	detergent	floor wax	broom
vacuum cleaner	trash can	pail	mops

OVEN

300 350
250   400
200   450
                500
Bake   Broil
OFF

Regular Cycle   Delicate Cycle
Permanent Press Cycle

Hot
Warm
Cool

WATER TEMPERATURE

147

1.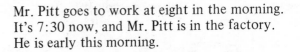

Mr. Pitt goes to work at eight in the morning. It's 7:30 now, and Mr. Pitt is in the factory. He is early this morning.

Mr. Spyros goes to work at 8:00 in the morning. It's 8:30 now, and he is not in the garage. He is late this morning.

Mr. and Mrs. Beck are going to dinner. Mr. Beck is ready. But Mrs. Beck is not ready.

2.

There's a shoe under the bed. It's Mr. Beck's left shoe.

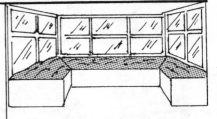

There's a seat under these windows. It's under them.

3.

The supermarket is between the bank and the drugstore.

The car is between the truck and the bus. It's between them.

4.

A: I'm going to Davidson's store. Where do I get off?
B: Get off at   the station.
                 the post office
                 this stop
                 Maple Street

A: I'm going to the hospital. Where do I get off?
B: Get off here. That's the hospital.

5.

Hurry up! We're late.

Are you ready?

O.K., I'm ready. Let's go.

Look out!

6.

1. Mr. and Mrs. Kent are going to Howard's Store this morning. There is a big sale there today.

2. "Are you ready, Ted? Hurry up! We'll be late."

3. "It's twenty to nine. Let's go."

4. "We're going to Howard's Store. Where do we get off?"

149

5. "Get off here. There's Howard's Store."

6. "Look out, Ted!"

7. "Here we are. It's not open. We're early."

8. Mrs. Kent is getting a shirt for her son.

9. She's getting a sweater for her daughter.

10. Mr. Kent is getting a tie. The ties are between the shirts and the men's sweaters.

11. "Where's my wallet? It's not in my pocket!"

12. "When did you have it?" "I had it on the bus."

13. "Here's your wallet." "Where was it?"

14. "It was under that table."

15. Mr. Kent has his wallet, but he hasn't any money now.

150

7. WORKING IN A FACTORY

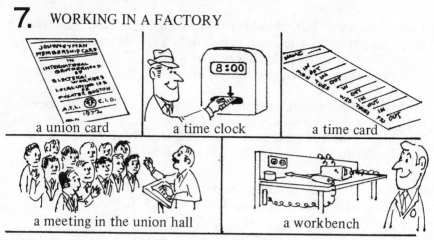

a union card   a time clock   a time card

a meeting in the union hall   a workbench

Mrs. Beck's brother Harry has a job in a factory. He is an *electrician*. That's his *union card*. He is in the Union of Electrical Workers of America. His union has *meetings* every month in the *union hall*.

Harry works at the factory from eight in the morning to four-forty in the afternoon, and he has forty minutes off for lunch. At eight in the morning, he puts his *time card* in the *time clock* and goes to his *workbench*. He is at the time clock every workday at eight. He comes to his work *on time*. At four-forty in the afternoon, he goes from his workbench to the time clock, puts his time card in, and goes to his car.

He is at the factory from eight to four-forty every workday; he works *union hours,* that is, forty hours a week for five days. He gets two weeks of vacation a year and six holidays a year.

This week's wages	$100.00
Last week's wages	95.00
Raise	$ 5.00

a raise of five dollars

Week's wages		$100.00
Deductions		
Union dues	1.00	
Insurance	4.50	
Taxes	14.00	
Social security	5.20	24.70
Take-home pay		$ 76.30

deductions and take-home pay

Today is *payday*. Harry has his *pay envelope* in his hand. This week his pay is $100.00. The one hundred dollars are his wages for the week's work. Last week his wages were $95.00. He got a *raise* of $5.00 this week. His wages are going up.

There are some *deductions* from his wages every week. $1.00 goes to his union for his *union dues* and $4.50 goes for *insurance*. Another $14.00 goes for *taxes* and $5.20 for social security (F.I.C.A.). This gives him deductions of $24.70 a week from his wages.

The *check* in his pay envelope this week is not a check for $100.00. It is a check for $76.30. His *take-home pay* is $76.30.

8. GOING TO THE BANK

X: Excuse me, please. Where is there a bank?
Y: There's one on Edison Street.

X: Excuse me, please. Where is there a bank?
Y: There's one on Edison Street, near White's garage.
X: Is it far from here?
Y: No, it's five minutes from here. You can take Bus 65.
X: Where do I get off?
Y: Get off at the supermarket. It's between the supermarket and the garage. There's your bus. Hurry.
X: Thank you.

9. THE HOLIDAY

It's the fourth of July. Mr. Beck is having a holiday. He and his wife Nelly are going to Cape Cod.

It's early in the morning. They are taking the morning bus to Falmouth.
"It's half past six, Nelly. Are you ready?"
"No, I'll be ready in ten minutes. Where are my white shoes?"
"They're there, under the bed."
"No, those are the old shoes. I want my new shoes."
"Oh, Nelly, take the brown or the black shoes, but hurry up. We'll be late for our bus!"

Mr. and Mrs. Beck went to the bus station in a taxi. They were at the station at ten to seven. Their bus is at eight.
"We're early, Robert!"
Mr. Beck went to the ticket office. He took his wallet from his pocket, but there wasn't any money in it.
"Where's my money, Nelly? I haven't any money!"

"It was on the telephone table this morning."
"On the telephone table?"
"Yes, under the address book."
"I'll take a taxi and get the money."
"But Robert, our bus goes in half an hour. You'll be late!"
"It's O.K., Nelly, I'll be here in twenty minutes."

It's ten to eight now. Mr. Beck got his money. He took another taxi to the bus station. He got the tickets at the ticket office, and he and Mrs. Beck are on the bus now.

Where can I get an a / some _____ ?

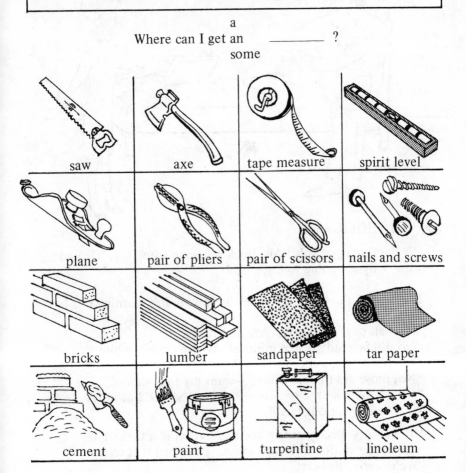

saw	axe	tape measure	spirit level
plane	pair of pliers	pair of scissors	nails and screws
bricks	lumber	sandpaper	tar paper
cement	paint	turpentine	linoleum

You're	hired. fired. promoted. laid off. transferred.